HUMANISM: A NEW RELIGION

CHARLES FRANCIS POTTER

HVMANISM
A NEW RELIGION

MCMXXX
SIMON AND SCHUSTER
NEW YORK

ALL RIGHTS RESERVED
COPYRIGHT, 1930, BY CHARLES FRANCIS POTTER
PUBLISHED BY SIMON AND SCHUSTER, INC.
37 WEST 57 STREET NEW YORK
PRINTED IN U. S. A. BY VAIL-BALLOU PRESS, BINGHAMTON
BOUND BY H. WOLFF EST., N. Y.
DESIGNED BY ANDOR BRAUN

LIBRARY
LUTHERAN SCHOOL OF THEOLOGY AT CHICAGO
1100 EAST 55th STREET
CHICAGO, ILLINOIS – 60615

CONTENTS

Preface vii

1 *The Advent of Humanism in Religion* . . 1
2 *What Is Humanism?* 14
3 *Are Humanists Atheists?* 46
4 *The Ancestry of Humanism* 61
5 *Was Jesus a Humanist?* 85
6 *Fundamentalism, Modernism, and Humanism* 92
7 *The Humanist Attitude Toward Prayer and Worship* 98
8 *The Problem of Immortality* 104
9 *Is Humanism a Religion?* 110
10 *What Inspiration Does Humanism Offer the Individual?* 115
11 *The Social Program of Humanism* . . . 123
12 *Humanism and the Religion of the Future* 127
   A Note on The Humanist Society . . . 131

PREFACE

The purpose of this book is to set forth as simply, yet as comprehensively as possible, the main outline and principal points of the new religion called Humanism. That there is need of such a summary is obvious to everyone who has made any attempt to get a clear conception of Humanism out of the confusion of conflicting and often erroneous current ideas concerning it. There is, of course, no definite system of belief held in common by all Humanists. Each Humanist may hold his own particular theory, but all Humanists are in general agreed not only upon the rejection of certain fundamental beliefs inherent in the old dogma but also upon the positive affirmation of certain other doctrines. I do not assert that all the statements concerning Humanism in this book are indorsed by all Humanists, but they do represent a consistent body of opinion.

This book was written in collaboration with my wife, Clara Cook Potter, to whom much of the thought and some of the phrasing is due.

1 THE ADVENT OF HUMANISM IN RELIGION

The humanistic trend of modern times has at last and inevitably reached religion. Inevitably, because man cannot endure the mental unbalance of retaining magic in his religion when he has banished it from all other departments of his life.

When man removed magic from alchemy and studied the laws of the elements, chemistry was born.

When he eliminated divination from astrology and learned the laws of the stars, astronomy rapidly developed.

And when he dares to excise the supernatural from religion and study the phenomena and laws of the religious life, similar progress will be made in that sphere.

Most unscientifically, theology, "the queen of the sciences," has begun with the unknown, has postulated the existence and attributes of God, and has thus based its whole structure on a supposition.

The new science of religion begins with the known phenomena, namely, the religious experience of man, and works toward the unknown. It admits that God is as yet unknown. In fact, if we are to have any science of religion at all, it must be agnostic about God. We may discover God some day, and we may not. To start with God is to beg the whole question and to place religion in the same category with alchemy and astrology.

Traditional ideas of God must be abandoned as inconsistent with advancing knowledge.

If any God is possible for modern men, it cannot be the tribal deity of Abraham, Isaac and Jacob, nor the Allah of Muhammad, nor the Heavenly Father of Jesus Christ. The only permissible God for men familiar with the facts of science differs so from the gods of the past that it is questionable whether it is right to use the name God at all. To realize that fact it is but necessary to eliminate all magic and supernaturalism from one's God-concept and then try to recognize what is left.

When a noted Modernist, still calling himself a Christian, says that he wants no God to nurse him here or give him a diadem hereafter, we heartily applaud him, but we point out at the same time that he has no right to claim that he still believes in the Christian God. If the gospel records and Christian history are worth anything at all, they indicate that the God who comforts here and gives a crown hereafter was the sort of God Jesus and his disciples believed in and the overwhelming majority of Christians ever since.

From such a God we must wean ourselves, hard though it may be.

The humanizing of religion has been postponed far too long, but there has been a reason for the delay. People have dreaded the very radical changes they knew would be necessary. It has seemed likely that the new religion will not be nearly as comfortable as the old: the Christian may even have to rely on himself in religion instead of leaning on the arms of Jesus.

Indeed it becomes increasingly evident that, while

the real values of the ideas, "God," "prayer," and "worship," may be retained, the present concepts, and perhaps even the words themselves, must sooner or later be abandoned.

So Humanism is not simply another denomination of Protestant Christianity; it is not a creed; nor is it a cult.

It is a new type of religion altogether.

It is a new way of looking at religion. You have to make over and broaden your definition of religion to get Humanism in at all, especially if you come from a Christian background. The Humanist splits the seams of all the old coats of religion when he tries them on. The new wine has burst the old wineskins.

The coming of Humanism is so great a change in religion that its significance will be apparent only as people become aware of its implications, probably a generation hence.

Apparently there has been a suddenness in the advent of Humanism. A few months ago one heard of it only in a very limited circle: today the word is on everybody's lips. Newspapers and magazines one picks up are full of it. Religious weeklies have little else in them these days save discussions of Humanism.

But the suddenness is only apparent. Humanism has been quietly growing in the minds of a few, waiting until the spread of scientific knowledge should prepare the way for its appearing. Persons familiar with trends in religious thought have for some time sensed a mighty change impending.

The revolution in religion they foresaw is here.

By revolution in religion we do not mean mere

reforms in religions, such as the reinterpreting of the cardinal tenets of orthodox Christianity in the light of modern thought, or the socializing of the religions which were formerly concerned only with the salvation of the individual.

Nor do we mean the Back to Jesus and Back to Buddha movements, nor the higher criticism of Bible, Koran, or Vedas.

These were but preparations for the revolution, shadows cast by the coming event.

The revolution is nothing less than the complete revaluation of religion itself on a humanistic basis rather than a theistic one. This revaluation is producing a religion so different in type from its predecessors that some critics claim it is no religion at all.

Christian Modernists are waking to the fact that Humanism is much farther ahead of them than they are in advance of orthodox Christianity. Put two marks an inch apart and another a mile away: the first two will represent Modernists and Fundamentalists and the third, Humanists.

As long as Modernists claim to be Christian, they cannot disavow supernaturalism, which is woven into the very fabric of Christianity. It cannot be withdrawn without destroying the goods.

Christianity has been patched many times where it has worn threadbare, so much so that it is difficult to detect the original cloth, but there comes a time when a garment cannot be mended again. A new coat must be made.

There is the sound of wild alarum in the Christian camp. The factions are trying to forget their differences to make common cause against the new enemy.

THE ADVENT OF HUMANISM IN RELIGION

Dr. Henry Sloan Coffin, president of Union Theological Seminary, New York, and one of the Modernist leaders, in an address last spring trumpeted a warning that Modernists and Fundamentalists must unite to fight the Humanists, "the scourge of Christendom."

But there is little danger for Humanism from united Christendom, which is but a mirage. Within six months Dr. Coffin was quarrelling with Bishop Manning, a Fundamentalist, over bones of contention so old they are mouldy, the questions of apostolic succession and the Lord's Supper!

A cartoonist could draw an eloquent picture,— the bishop in full regalia on one side of the communion table shaking his fist at the irate professor in cap and gown on the other side. In their scuffle they have knocked the Holy Grail off the table and it rolls neglected at their feet.

And even if Fundamentalist and Modernist Protestants could agree, Christendom would be far from united. Neither Dr. Coffin's nor Bishop Manning's orders would be recognized as valid in the Roman Catholic department of Christianity, which in turn is looked down upon as an heretical schism by the oldest division of Christendom, the Greek or Eastern Church, which calls itself proudly, "The Holy Orthodox Catholic and Apostolic Church."

The hope of a united Christian church saving the world is rapidly being abandoned, not only because Christendom persistently refuses to be united, but also because Christianity is so impregnated with supernaturalism as to be irreconcilable with the scientific method by which man is solving his modern problems.

HUMANISM: A NEW RELIGION

There are sixty million people in the United States alone who are not on the lists of adherents of the Christian churches and the Jewish synagogues. They are outside organized Christianity and Judaism. The figures seem startling, but they are easily verifiable by subtracting from the approximately one hundred and twenty millions in this country the fifty millions claimed by the churches and synagogues, and allowing ten millions for the Christian Scientists and New Thought groups.

These sixty millions are not to be reckoned as not desiring any religion. It is probable that most of them are simply dissatisfied with the religions they have known, the religions which emphasize the supernatural. They have tried many cults and faddish movements, one after another, only to leave them in disgust at puerilities far worse than those of Christianity.

To these people who are seeking a satisfactory religion for today Humanism comes as something long sought and almost despaired of. The letter-files of Humanist preachers are growing plethoric with correspondents' expressions of delight at having found "at last a religion I can believe and live by," "a common sense religion for today," and "an inspiring faith for modern folk."

Humanism is still very young, but its adherents exhibit the enthusiasm which characterizes the rise of a new religion. And there is a sanity and wholesomeness about it which render its followers immune to the fanatic excesses which have been exhibited in some religions.

From California to New York, and even in India and Japan, Humanist groups are in process of for-

THE ADVENT OF HUMANISM IN RELIGION

mation, and every week brings fresh news of the growth of the new movement.

Not all these groups agree in all details of belief and practice, but certain common elements appear. One notices in all of them, naturally, an emphasis on the value of sincerity and a corresponding scorn of hypocrisy. They all stress the importance of living the good life here and now, rather than worrying much about what is to come afterward. They repeat frequently the need of self-development by the individual and lay great emphasis on social cooperation and a sense of social responsibility. They find inspiration in contemplating the upward sweep of evolution and the noble lives of the great heroes of human progress.

The point upon which they are unanimous and most insistent is the rejection of belief in the supernatural.

This is the great dividing line between Humanism and all other religions, in America, at any rate. The gap between Humanism and the other religions is so great that very frequently Humanists are charged with being atheists.

Atheist is simply a convenient derogatory epithet applied by the orthodox to the unorthodox. The person using it assumes that his god is the only true god.

It is rather amusing to a Humanist to be called an atheist by a Christian, for when Christianity first appeared, its opponents among the old religions of the Roman Empire called the Christians "atheists." When Polycarp, Bishop of Smyrna, and his little band of fellow Christians were harried from their hiding places and burned in the arena in 155 A. D., the cry of the mob was, "Down with the atheists!"

When Theists discover that Humanists do not worship any god, they are all the more ready to apply to the newcomers the sobriquet "atheist," for they assume, with a beautiful *non sequitur* in logic, that all who are not Theists must be atheists. Humanists take the only logical position in an age of science, and are agnostics. They do not say there is a God: they do not say there is not a God: they say simply that they do not know.

While Humanists are not atheists, neither are they Theists, for the Theist believes in God, and the word "God" means, to the great majority of people anyway, a supernatural being.

But religion is wider than supernaturalism. As scientists who specialize in studying the phenomena of religion are pointing out, there are wide areas of religion where the supernatural does not enter at all.

Philosophy was once largely metaphysics, but the metaphysical element has been left to one side in several recent systems of philosophy. In fact, there are wide areas in philosophy where metaphysics does not enter at all. It is just as inaccurate to say that religion without the supernatural is not religion as it is to say that philosophy without metaphysics is not philosophy at all.

Recent definitions of religion by expert students of religion are much broader than those formerly taught. Contrast Allan Menzies' definition in his *History of Religion* (1895), "Religion is the worship of higher powers from a sense of need" with that of E. S. Ames in *The Psychology of Religious*

Experience (1910), "Religion is the consciousness of the highest social values."

Or take Immanuel Kant's famous definition in his *Critique of Practical Reason* (1788) "Religion is the recognition of all duties as divine commands" and compare it with A. Eustace Haydon's in *The Quest of the Ages* (1929), "Religion is the shared quest of the good life."

According to Kant and Menzies, representatives of the older type of thought, Humanism would hardly be called a religion, but under the definitions of Ames and Haydon it certainly would.

Religion is the attempt to unify one's personality and relate it to the world without. Hitherto men have thought that this process necessarily involved the worship and propitiation of certain supernatural beings, but the advance of science has made such a belief seem rather naive, almost childish.

The really revolutionary character of Humanism is best seen when one realizes that Humanists not only do not consider belief in the supernatural necessary in religion, but even hold that today such a belief may defeat the purpose of religion. For if religion seeks to unify the personality and relate it to the world without, any belief which hinders either part of the process is detrimental.

Now a belief in supernatural beings is quite foreign to the modern man's understanding of the scheme of things. His knowledge of science prevents him from finding any room in the world outside himself or the world of personality within himself for either gods or demons. Such beings simply cannot exist for him, in the sense in which they existed for the men of the pre-scientific age.

In Bible times, men could believe in gods and demons: they knew no better way of explaining certain phenomena. Jesus believed that the way the earth and man came into being was by direct creation by the hand of Jehovah. He believed that disease was due to demon-possession. He believed that wrong thoughts were whisperings of Satan. He believed that good thoughts and good deeds were due to the presence of God or the Holy Spirit within him.

The man of the twentieth century who is familiar with even the commonplaces of scientific truth classifies all the creation stories, whether in Hebrew literature or in the lore of the South Sea Islands, as primitive myths. He accepts evolution as the method by which the earth and man arrived at their present state. He knows that disease is due to germs: he has seen them through a high-school microscope. And he knows that it is just as inaccurate to ascribe his good thoughts, aspirations, and actions to a god as it is to blame the devil for his bad thoughts and deeds.

Such primitive ideas do not aid a man when he seeks today to get a unified view of his life and his relations to others and to nature. They only confuse him and defeat his highest purposes. He cannot reconcile an ancient religion with his modern life.

And when some earnest Theist informs him that if he does not believe in the supernatural he can have no religion, he decides that he must give up religion in order to preserve his intellectual and emotional and moral integrity.

With the coming of Humanism, however, the modern man finds a religion which does fit in with his scheme of things. Not that he welcomes it as an easy let-down in his standards, permitting him to take a moral vacation and to do as he pleases. Far from it, for while Humanism is easier to understand and believe, it is harder to live by, for it requires more personal consecration and devotion to the highest ideals and a deeper sense of social responsibility than does orthodox religion.

Long ago, centuries before Christ, when philosophic humanism had developed in the magnificent Greek civilization, Socrates counselled every man he met: "Know thyself." In the intervening centuries, however, man has exerted his powers mainly to discover the world outside. Only recently has he turned his instruments upon himself. In years to come, the twentieth century will probably be known as the era of the discovery of human personality.

Recent researches in psychology have also prepared the way for the coming of Humanism, a positive constructive religion built upon man's faith in his own powers. If Humanists were to make a creed, the first article would be: "I believe in Man."

To some, such a statement sounds sacrilegious, because they have for so long been accustomed to the idea of the Fall of Man and his inherent depravity, and have repeated so many times the false aphorism: "Human nature never changes." They have thus created in their own minds a barrier to belief in the limitless possibilities of mankind.

There is good scientific justification for believing that man is really just beginning his career upon this earth and that a million years or more of development, mentally, morally, and spiritually, lie before him. What may not be accomplished if man dares to believe in his own future and to take his vast responsibilities to those who come after him more seriously than has been possible when religion has centered his attention on "otherworldliness"!

Man's recent accomplishments, however, in the spheres of radio communication and the conquest of the air, have gone far to create in him a confidence in his own latent powers.

It becomes immediately apparent that the chief concern of Humanism is to release the pent-up reservoir of human energy, to explore the uncharted territory of the mind, and to raise to its highest efficiency the entire personality.

Therefore Humanists are not only opposed to all movements, institutions and practices, however religiously sanctioned, which tend to cramp and confine the human personality and to prevent its proper development, but they are also actively engaged in helping those movements which tend to release, develop and expand the life of man.

If there be detected in any Humanist a seeming antipathy towards the older religions, it is due not to lack of appreciation of the values conserved in those religions, but to an impatience with the church as an institution which has so frequently stood athwart the progress of the human spirit.

Protestantism, according to its own ablest exponents, is disintegrating, and is spending much of its strength in civil war. Catholicism is essentially medieval in character, and, largely because its present leaders are not as wise in recognizing the trend of the times as were its early founders, will probably eventually cease to interest those familiar with modern scientific discoveries.

Not only is the average man dissatisfied with orthodox Christianity, but his brothers in every country of the world show a similar impatience with existing religions of revelation and supernaturalism. The time has come for men of every race to shake themselves free from inhibitions and taboos, and make a new faith for the new age.

To men and women of today, Humanism offers inspiration and a program. Here they may study their own personalities until they become familiar not only with their own virtues but also with their tendencies to seek the lesser good. They may plan their own continued education, consulting with those who can help them. By belief in themselves, by self-discipline, and by patient earnest effort, inspired by contemplation of the beautiful, the good and the true, they may build personalities of character and influence, and cooperate intelligently with all those agencies working for human betterment.

In the challenge to make the world better here and now, the Humanist will find all the thrills which formerly intrigued the seekers of celestial bliss in the hereafter. Heaven as a reward concerns him even less than hell as a punishment. Not that the Humanist is necessarily unconcerned with the great problem of immortality. He simply approaches it in another and more scientific way. The possible continuance of personality he believes more likely to find its explanation by scientific research and the study of the personality itself than by any revelation from the skies made to favored prophets.

2 WHAT IS HUMANISM?

Humanism is faith in the supreme value and self-perfectibility of human personality.

By *faith* is meant belief so strongly held as to influence all decisions.

By *supreme value* is meant that there is nothing else in the universe so important and that all things else are of value only as they contribute to it.

By *self-perfectibility* is meant that the ability and desire to improve are within.

By *human personality* is meant that unity of qualities and powers making up the self-recognizing, self-directing, self-giving individual.

The self-perfectibility of human personality is to be conceived socially as well as individually because the individual obviously cannot improve unless society does, nor society unless the individual does.

The definition of Humanism given above may be expanded to read:

Humanism is the conviction that personality is the explanation of the universe, that man himself is the highest manifestation of this personality, and that the powers resident in the individual and society are sufficient to ensure progress toward an ideal society of ideal persons.

In the statement that personality is the explanation of the universe, there are implicit three ideas, namely,

(1) That the universe has meaning
(2) which is discoverable by man
(3) as the supremacy of personality.

That the universe has meaning is the primary assumption of all thought. It is the starting-point of science as well as of religion.

Humanism agrees with science in the second of these three ideas, namely, that man can discover this meaning. In this, Humanism differs from Theism, which has maintained that the meaning of the universe is not discovered by man but revealed by God.

Through his scientific study of the universe man has arrived at the theory of evolution. In this also, the Humanist finds himself at variance with many Theists. It will be remembered that the theory of evolution found its bitterest and most persistent opponents among the theistic religionists. Only gradually and with reluctance has orthodoxy readjusted its theology to make room in it for the theory of evolution. There are many Theists today who believe in evolution, but they have had to make over their idea of God considerably. Indeed, they have not yet succeeded in making a satisfactory adjustment. It is still to be seen whether or not Theism will survive the shock which the theory of evolution has given it.

When the evolution of the world and of life thereon is viewed as a whole, there seems to be indicated a development toward man as the highest type. When matter took on life, there began a march toward man through countless slowly changing forms of living beings. In man's own physical and mental constitution are reminders of the long struggle upward. Man himself is the epitome of evolution and all nature points toward him as the justification of the experimentation. Vegetable and animal life affords him food in constantly increasing variety as he learns to enter into his heritage of sustenance. The whole earth is his, and he is adapting it and making it over to his needs.

This is not to say that man is perfect, far from it. Those who are inclined to pessimism and cynicism can find ample material for criticism of man and his ways. But man is to be judged not by looking at immature, incomplete personalities, but by the higher specimens, the leaders of the spear-head of progress. Just as the uncouth dinosaurs represent by-products of evolution, so also many human beings, unlovely in character, must be looked on as necessary waste in experimentation.

Human personality at its best, imperfect as it is, is yet sufficiently worthy and admirable to justify the universe. Of course, that statement is still debatable, but, after all, it is a matter of faith, and faith in man is the central doctrine of Humanism. It is a challenge to all men to dare to believe that human personality is of supreme value.

The second part of our definition of Humanism, namely, the self-perfectibility of human personality, depends for its acceptance very evidently upon an analysis of human personality. The reluctance of many to believe that man can, without supernatural aid, improve himself and the race is largely due to an underestimate of the value of personality in man.

This underestimate is, in turn, due to an overestimate of the power of the personality of God. But when it is recognized that the very stress laid by Theists on the power of God is really a testimony to the power

WHAT IS HUMANISM?

of man, we have further support for believing in man's ability to make his own progress.

There is no doubt whatever that man has in the past been conscious of an access of personal power after a period of prayer. Naturally, his training having been theistic, he has attributed that power to God. But he has really been deriving that power from himself. By meditation, quiet thought, high resolve, combined with an analysis of the problem facing him, he has risen from his knees a stronger person. He has called on his own reserves.

The fact that he has attributed that access of power to a supernatural God does not prove that the strength really came from God. It only shows that the man praying has not realized the extent of his own conscious and subconscious powers. Stored within him is a vast fund of racial experience, interpreted and increased by his own previous individual experience. Only as he "takes time to think" does he become aware of all the possibilities in the case. Where before he was sure there was no way out of his trouble, his period of calm consideration of the problem has revealed to him that there is a solution.

To a simple person, entirely unaware of thought-processes and frequently ignorant of the fact that he has a subconscious memory, the coming of an answer to his problem has seemed like a message from the sky. God gets the credit for what man has done himself, and if anyone tries to reason with man and tell him the real source of his new-found strength, it seems to the Theist a species of blasphemy.

This is not to identify God with the subconscious. It is simply to point out that to a person unacquainted with psychology, the theory that God has answered his prayer seems reasonable.

For so many centuries now man has been told that he is unworthy and vile by nature, weak, helpless and filled with sin, that if he is told by a psychologist that the prayer-answers have come from within himself, he replies that it is impossible. And when a Humanist asserts that human personality is self-perfectible, he meets with a storm of misunderstanding and incredulity.

The sad situation is that man does not know himself, does not understand his own possibilities, and therefore blindly continues to look outside for the aid that is already available within him.

The message needed by man today is a call to study and develop his own personality. And this is the gospel of Humanism.

When we define Humanism as faith in the supreme value and self-perfectibility of human personality, it is necessary for us to define and analyze human personality, and that is our present task.

It is difficult to define personality, a difficulty which it shares with all elemental things, largely because we cannot get outside to look at it. For conscious beings to define their own consciousness is a baffling task, but it is becoming less difficult since psychology has come to the aid of philosophy. It still requires considerable mental balance to objectify one's subjective states.

The difficulty of defining personality is increased by the fact that the word in its modern sense is comparatively new, and its content growing and not yet fixed. Negatively, a person is a human being as distinguished from a thing or an animal. Yet there are evidences that some animals have characteristics which are partly personal. As for the positive definition, it is still in the process of being worked out. We are gradually determining what are the essential qualities of personality. Psychology is, comparatively speaking, a very youthful science, and its schools are at variance with each other. Philosophy and religion are beginning to realize that they are somewhat dependent upon the findings of psychology, and since those findings are far from being determined, both philosophy and religion are in a state of indecision and confusion.

Another related difficulty in defining personality is the fact that no complete or perfect person is at hand for us to examine. Man is slowly growing personal and it is hard for him to visualize his distant goal. By the time a given ideal is realized a higher one has taken its place. There are on the earth now races and individuals in all stages of development and it is very debatable which type of person is farthest along on the road toward the desirable person of the future.

In spite of these and other difficulties in the way of arriving at a complete definition, however, we have made sufficient progress to outline a preliminary one. Men have studied the growing personalities of others, and have compared the knowledge thus gained with the results of self-examination. They have noted certain repeated factors, certain common qualities and modes of behavior. To an extent, it is possible to assign some types of human beings to a place nearer the animals and others to a higher place in the scale. This gives ground for a tentative definition of personality.

Immanuel Kant is the thinker from whom dates

HUMANISM: A NEW RELIGION

the modern appreciation of the importance of personality. Before him there were men who contributed to the concept, notably Augustine, Descartes, and Leibnitz, but it was Kant who developed the ideas of self-consciousness and self-determination as attributes of personality. A person is therefore an end in himself. He is both the source and end of thought and conduct.

One of the notable thinkers on the problem of personality was J. R. Illingworth. His Bampton Lectures (1894) on *Personality Human and Divine* were an argument for the personality of God. In the course of the first lecture he defined personality as "the name of the unity in which all a man's attributes and functions meet, making him an individual self." That definition might then be simplified into a tentative one.

A personality is that unity of qualities and powers which we call the self.

These qualities and powers might be termed the elements of personality. They consist of Kant's self-consciousness and self-determination plus a third, self-giving. And we prefer to call the first two self-recognition and self-direction.

When we speak of self-recognition, self-direction, and self-giving, we do not wish to imply that it is only upon the self that these powers act. They have to do with environment as well. Self-recognition presupposes an awareness of that which is not self. Self-direction needs a phenomenal world of matter through which the self shall make its path. And the giving of self implies a recipient of the gift. It is upon the self, however, that the personality does its greatest work.

All three qualities, self-recognition, self-direction,

and self-giving are important in a well-rounded personality. The proper balance of the three is also essential.

Some personalities do not contain the third element, self-giving, to any appreciable degree; some seem to lack in self-direction, and no human personality has even the first fully developed. We have stated them in the order of their development in the individual as well as in the race, and we shall consider them in that order.

The beginnings of the personal process are vague, casual, and difficult to delineate. The first indication of self-recognition in a child or a primitive savage may possibly be found in the use of some form of the personal pronoun "I," but we must go some distance back into the animal world before we can assert confidently that there is no distinction between subject and object. This distinction is what marks the dawn of consciousness of self. There probably was a long period when the high animal which evolved into man hovered on the edge of self-recognition. The degree of intelligence necessary before that animal could become conscious of himself is difficult to measure.

Self-recognition, the knowledge that one is a self, a being able to act on his environment intelligently and to know that he is acting on it and is distinct from it—this is the first and distinguishing mark of personality. It is a necessary element in personality, no matter how many others may be added to it.

Self-consciousness has been analyzed as containing two features, self-grasp and self-estimate, but self-recognition would seem to include them both and to be preferable to self-consciousness, for two reasons. First, self-consciousness has today the secondary meaning of "conscious of oneself as the object of the observation of others," thus connoting embarrassment; and, second, the word self-consciousness is tautological because the word consciousness itself means knowledge of "what passes inwardly," or "knowledge of one's own existence, condition, sensations, mental operations, acts, etc." Since consciousness means knowledge of self, self-consciousness is needless repetition. Consequently we prefer the word self-recognition.

The moment a being awakes to his self-hood, he is a person and on the road to becoming fully personal. He has frequent relapses, and in one sense is only occasionally personal. This self-recognition, which permits him to be classed with persons, may be but a dim differentiation of himself from his surroundings; with many people it proceeds very little further. They speak of their bodies as themselves. They become so attached to one environment and one group of friends that they are at a loss when it is necessary for them to fit their personality into another neighborhood. They had depended so much upon the group and the familiar surroundings that they had almost forgotten that they were individuals.

But in some cases the recognition of self progresses to remarkable degrees. A genius is usually a man who has recognized and appreciated his own personality to the extent of daring to invest infinite work in it. A certain amount of conceit, or, at least, pride, seems to have been characteristic of many of the great men of the earth. And the humble ones took considerable pride in their humility. At the very least, success depends upon knowing one's self rather well, both one's good points and one's weaknesses. In the great religious geniuses, self-exploration reached the point where the man discovered what he sometimes called a "divine" element within himself. Whether or not this divine spark ever amounts to anything depends usually upon its cultivation by the self, with or without the assistance of others. The religious consciousness is remarkably sensitive and responsive to careful attention.

A recognition of one's powers and possibilities is extremely important if life is to be lived in all its richness. There are many cramped and thwarted lives which might have been glorious had there not been a reticence and bashfulness about self-examination and analysis. Even where life has reached middle-age without any worth-while accomplishment, a searching appraisal of one's inner resources may result in a late but transfiguring out-flowering of unsuspected powers. If our educators can be brought to realize that self-recognition is the very foundation of personality development and therefore the prerequisite of all education, civilization will move forward with hitherto unknown ease and rapidity.

It is not simply that self-recognition should begin early in the individual; it should be continued through life. Every year fresh possibilities appear within us, only to die still-born because we are too busy to do the most important thing, to know ourselves.

Introspection is popularly supposed to lead to morbidity. That is because most self-examination in the past has been conducted under the auspices of a self-deprecatory theism. Men have been bidden to ponder on their guilt and have been taught to sing, "Lord, my sins have been many, like the sands of the sea." Conscience has been considered a condemnatory organ.

Humanism urges men to discover their own good qualities and to note their inadequacies only to guard against them or to remedy them.

Nor does Humanism make the mistake of many who have fled the morbid self-condemnation of revival Christianity only to fall into the snare of an over-optimistic appraisal of one's powers. Whoso teaches that man, any man, can do anything if he only believes he can, is a blind leader of the blind. True self-appraisal reveals one's limitations as well as one's possibilities.

Human personality is self-perfectible because in the long run man has or may develop enough intelligence to estimate his powers accurately. By the use of his abilities to their reasonable limit he will find that new powers are developed. That is the teaching of evolution itself. To him that hath, and uses what he hath, shall be given what he as yet hath not.

Self-recognition, then, to sum up briefly, is the earliest and most fundamental element of personality, yet may continue to grow almost indefinitely. The more developed it is, the more man is able to shape his own destiny. So self-recognition leads directly to self-direction, the second of the three elements of human personality.

It is not long after man first learns to recognize himself as apart from matter (although related to it) before he finds that he has, to a certain extent, power over matter. In spite of the fact that he frequently finds himself the sport of cruel circumstances, which he clumsily tries to propitiate, he is delighted at his growing power over his surroundings. His knife, his arrow, his boat, all represent triumphs over limiting environment.

As mankind rises in civilization, victories of self-direction increase. He can go, more frequently, in the direction in which he wishes to go. The mountain no longer forbids his progress for he bores through it or flies over it and goes straight to his goal. He finds that he has added to his self-recognition the power of self-direction. Free-will triumphs over determinism. Indeed, he comes to see that "will is the very core and essence of personality." With increased powers of determining his path comes confidence and he dares the hitherto impossible. He wills to succeed and his measure of success is astounding. He masters engineering problems of vastness and intricacy. He learns arts requiring deftness of touch, delicacy of perception and patience unlimited.

Self-direction and its concomitant self-control reach such a high point in some persons that they dominate their environment and leave the marks of their personality apparent to all. Their actions are characteristic; their deeds are recognizable by others as theirs indubitably. The great artist need not sign his canvas. He has achieved freedom and is self-determined, in one direction at least. Self-direction in a well-developed form is the mark of a master among men. The self-directed personality is a continual inspiration to his fellows. He constantly points them to the self-perfectibility of human personality.

It is in the art of living that man faces his greatest problems. The successful artist may be a poor husband or a bad neighbor. It is when self-direction is concerned with self-development that the man is tested. It is easier to manage tools than one's own temperament. Character-building is harder than house-building.

Face to face with a moral decision, a boy chooses the right path, and discovers that the surmounted crisis is a building-stone in character. Immediately other choices present themselves and he is soon busy with the problem of self-development which will occupy him all his life. He is engaged from childhood in solving problems and reconciling contradictions.

Growth comes as man is forced to extend his range of thinking by reducing all his impressions to an ever-enlarging unity, which is his personality. Unless he stifles it, that divine element within himself, that dæmon of Socrates, urges him on and on. His self-recognition and self-control increase and he grows in personality. The unorganized parts of his personality swing into place as he gradually subordinates the lower to the higher within himself.

He finds himself to be the player, the game-board, the opponent, the game, and finally, the victory—or the defeat. It is all within his own personality. To be sure, his relations with other men have a mighty influence upon him; no personality can develop alone; but his personality very early and very persistently exercises a selective judgment upon the chance material brought into the inner workshop of his senses.

The first mark of personality, self-recognition, is an activity of man's intellect: the second element, self-direction, is an activity of the will. We commonly divide a person's mental equipment into intellect, will, and sensibility, with the corresponding attributes of intelligence, power, and affection. Our next natural step, then, is to find the third mark of personality, self-giving, arising from the region of the affections.

At an early stage in his self-development the person usually has a strong desire to communicate his personality to others. Of course speech itself is that, but there is an urge for self-expression which is not satisfied by mere speech. The desire for self-communication is the source of creative art, and the personality of the artist grows by expression. It is also the cause of the development of the family.

It is true that one cannot share his immediate ego with even his closest friend, much as he or the friend may wish it, yet he finds himself growing the more he enters into other life. He increases his personality by giving himself away in creative activities or in love for others. "At his minimum he is almost mere exclusiveness and antagonism. At his maximum he is one with the greatest and widest forms of life." (Bosanquet, *The Value and Destiny of the Individual*, p. 40.)

The person who found himself growing by correct moral choices finds that that growth is increased by self-giving to others. Furthermore, he faces those moral crises in the light of the needs of his social group, and not only refrains from eating the meat which may cause his brother to stumble, but uses for the positive betterment of his brother the money which the meat would have cost. He cannot call himself saved until his brothers are. His ideal becomes not merely the development of his own individual personality but the growth of all personalities. He may even find himself called on to lose his own life for the betterment of his brothers. The more he schools himself to take the larger social outlook, the more he is conscious of the growth of his own personality in richness and worth. That is, he finds himself becoming increasingly personal. His self-recognition and his self-direction are called into the service of his self-giving, and his self-giving reveals to him a deeper knowledge of himself and a wider field for self-direction. Thought, will, and feeling interblend and fuse in the higher operations of a developed personality.

Now, by some, the third element of personality which we have called self-giving is called self-sacrifice, which has frequently been lauded as the highest Christian virtue. Self-sacrifice has been deemed to have a peculiarly valuable quality, probably because the self-sacrifice of Christ on the cross is the central Christian doctrine.

Our recognition of the claims of the wider personality may sometimes call for the sacrifice of self, but not frequently. Humanism would find higher value in social service than in vicarious suffering, for the suffering is incidental and accomplishes little in itself.

It is true that our pain may excite, first, interest, then shame, and finally, repentance, in the one for whom we are suffering, as when the father punishes himself instead of the guilty child, while the child looks on. To force a child to witness the vicarious suffering of a loved parent is poor ethics and poorer pedagogy. If there must be punishment, it had better be given directly. Even a child will recognize that justice is thus better served.

So also, salvation from sin through the vicarious sacrifice of Christ on Calvary is losing its appeal today, not because men are growing worse but because they judge by higher ethical standards than formerly. A more acute ethical consciousness perceives that in-

WHAT IS HUMANISM?

telligent self-giving is better than self-sacrifice for others. The whole vicarious atonement idea is built upon an ancient idea that without the shedding of blood there can be no remission of sin. Today that idea seems a somewhat morbid superstition. Bloodshed is a sign of blunder whether in international relations or on an operating table in a hospital. The old chirurgeon's main business was blood-letting: the modern surgeon takes pride in performing a major operation with the minimum of blood loss.

There may be, and there frequently is, salvation by social service without any suffering, vicarious or otherwise. Indeed, the social worker uses intelligence to avoid suffering as far as possible, both for self and others. A self-made martyr, walking on spikes, or shutting himself in a hermit's hut, or wearing a hairshirt full of vermin, was wont to receive the admiration of former ages. Today, however, such a sufferer is hardly to be classed as an ideal citizen. Indeed, considering the fact that the other citizens are taxed in one way or another to support him in his orgy of self-torture, he is rather to be reckoned as distinctly undesirable.

Self-sought suffering in order to be thought holy, or even to excite sympathy, is one of the most despicable attitudes a man may take. It is a morbid inversion of values. The duty of all who seek a high religion is to discourage rather than encourage asceticism of the martyr type. Self-sacrifice of that sort is the very opposite of self-giving, for it demands sympathy rather than gives it, and is a social liability rather than a social asset.

If, in the course of duty, suffering comes, it is to be accepted and endured, but only temporarily. Always the Humanist who suffers is planning that the suffering may not occur again, either for himself or for others. Pain of any sort is a sign of maladjustment and not a sign either of the wrath or the love of a supernatural deity. Pain is a social warning and not a religious accolade.

The difference in attitude between a Humanist and an orthodox Theist toward the matter of suffering can be stated by saying that when a Humanist suffers, he has no illusion that he is expiating by pain for either his own sins or another's, and thereby satisfying the demands of a supervising deity. The Humanist will willingly suffer, however, that another or many others may not have to, or if the suffering is necessary for the accomplishment of some desirable end.

Self-giving, then, is not to be identified with self-sacrifice: it is a larger virtue of wider worth. Intelligent self-giving is the highest aim of the mature personality.

It should not be supposed that self-giving is entirely social in its aim. The giver of self for the benefit of others derives benefit himself in several ways. He benefits from the fact that his donation to the public good makes a better community for him to live in; for instance, the man who gives of his time, energy and ability to secure for his town a better water system himself drinks purer water as a minor reward. But he also derives other advantages. His community thinks more of him and his circle of friends increases. Better yet, he respects himself more and gains courage for other social tasks. He also appreciates more the work of others who are devoting their talents to community improvement. In every

WHAT IS HUMANISM?

way his self-giving has carried him further along the road toward higher personality.

Self-giving has another aspect, entirely removed from social benefits. Self-expression is self-giving. The artist expresses himself in a painting; the composer, in a musical piece; the poet, in his stanzas. The public does receive the benefit of these productions, but the real artist does not have the audience in mind. He gives forth the thing that is in him. If he refuses it utterance, he loses the growth into higher personality which is the real reward of all self-givers. Creative effort marks the climax of personal development.

A machine age denies to many the opportunity for creative activity and stunts many a growing personality. Yet for such there are opportunities for self-giving which will compensate. No one is shut out from the higher planes of life. It is true that access to modes of self-expression is easier for some than others, but the increase of educational opportunities is opening vistas to mental shut-ins. No one is too poor to share his inner life with someone. There are more who deny themselves the joy of self-giving because of apathy and mental laziness than are denied that pleasure by circumstance.

There are others whose lives are incomplete because they limit their expression to one field. When expression is hindered in their chosen art or profession, they wither mentally. Versatility is not an accident: it is an accomplishment. It is a good thing to have many strings to one's bow. The value of learning a foreign language is not so much the gain in linguistic ability as in the extension of personality to include new thought forms and modes of expression. Travel widens mental horizons. Good books, carefully read and pondered upon, feed the personal life of the reader with the stored-up life reactions of great personalities. Said Milton, "A good book is the precious life-blood of a master spirit, embalmed and treasured up on purpose to a life beyond life."

From varied sources the pursuer of his own better self selects that which furthers his quest. He must place himself in a way to receive the impressions which later come forth to color and enrich his expressions. All the heritage from the past and all the teeming life of the present is his hunting-ground for the material for personality-making.

Yet all search for such material is vain unless there be developed the capacity for digesting and assimilating it. We are not part of all we have met unless we make it part of us. "A strong personality," said Dr. George Cross, the theologian, in a lecture on personality which unfortunately was not printed, "is one who has focussed many modes of purposing, thinking and willing in his own life."

It is surprising how many people are living in only one part of their personalities. A "well-rounded life" is a common phrase for something we seldom see and yet which would be common enough if religion became a matter of personality culture. There is enough latent power in human personality to transform itself and the world if men would only free themselves from the sense of inferiority and insignificance and the fears which Theism has bred in them through centuries.

Humanism calls to men to recognize their potential power, to choose and direct their own paths, to enter deeply and richly into life's experiences, and to give forth freely to others of the wealth within them.

WHAT IS HUMANISM?

Humanism is faith in the supreme value and self-perfectibility of human personality.

We have been concerned thus far in this chapter with the positive setting forth of what Humanism is. There remains to be shown what it is not, for the presentation of the negative side is necessary in every complete definition. That can best be done by contrasting Humanism with the established religion, Theism.

Humanism is belief in man.

Theism is faith in God.

Humanism bases its belief on the natural.

Theism founds its faith on the supernatural.

Theism regards the supernatural as beyond the comprehension of man and therefore to be worshipped.

Humanism denies the existence of any realm outside the field of cause and effect, and holds that what is called the supernatural is only the not-yet-understood natural. The Humanist questions the value of worshipping the not-yet-understood. It is too dangerously near to the ignorance and superstition of the early Theists.

From the dim region of the so-called supernatural with its not-yet-discovered laws, strange influences have always affected man's life, bringing to him harm as well as good. So man has always stood in awe and fear of the unknown. He could not tell how the unseen forces would act, so he attempted to propitiate the great uncomprehended. He personified and worshipped these powers, begging them to send blessing rather than bane.

Most early tribes feared the strange mysterious

force which manifested itself in thunder and lightning. Yahweh, Zeus, Jupiter, Thor, and Tlaloc were gods who spoke in thunderous tones and smote hapless mortals with the lightning of their wrath, and therefore commanded the worship and sacrifices of the trembling Theists of the time.

More efficacious today, however, than prayer and sacrifice in averting the lightning, even from churches, is the lightning-rod, an invention of that eighteenth century Humanist, Benjamin Franklin. Instead of worshipping electricity, we now use its light, heat and power to make the earth more comfortable for men.

Humanists hold that this process is typical. Man's attitude toward forces he does not understand should not be that of fear and worship, but that of curiosity and inquiry. Franklin's kite is an excellent symbol for Humanism. Its framework was a wooden cross, but what a different thing is Humanism from classical Christianity!

Instead of a cross on which a man is stretched in agony to appease the wrath of an angry sky-god, behold a cross on which is spread a silken covering to carry it skyward to trap electric force for the service of man. One symbol typifies salvation by sacrifice; the other, service by science.

The men of long ago, and not so very long ago at that, feared thunder as they feared comets: such portents revealed the anger of God. To laugh in a thunder-storm was a particularly daring form of blasphemy.

But today a high-school physics student will refer to thunder as a steep compression wave, and smile at mention of any theological implications.

There was a very genuine fear exhibited by certain old folk when the first airplanes appeared. Some expected that the end of the world would come. To them the bold pioneer navigators of the airplanes were literally "flying in the face of Providence." If God had intended men to fly, would He not have equipped them with wings? Was not the sky God's domain and would He not jealously resent any impudent human intruders?

But one by one the fears of man have yielded to his growing knowledge. The area of the supernatural has been gradually reduced, and with increasing rapidity these latter years. It is not to be expected that young engineers who can photo-map Olympus and Sinai from an airplane will be very ardent Theists.

Epidemics of dread disease, formerly looked upon as pestilences sent by a displeased deity to plague and punish disobedient men, have been studied by brave men who have eaten of the forbidden fruit of the tree of knowledge. The cause of the disease has been discovered and removed, and thus another argument of ancient Theism rendered innocuous.

It is reported that the sanitary engineers cleaning up the Panama Canal zone by destroying the disease-bearing mosquitoes had difficulty in persuading a priest to remove from the doorway of a church a basin of holy-water, although it was alive with larvæ. From the view-point of Humanism the engineers were engaged on a more sacred mission than the priest.

Not only have astronomical phenomena and pestilential diseases been removed from the realm of the supernatural, but the mental and physical conditions of man himself which were once considered indubitable proofs of the presence in man of demons or gods or holy ghosts are also seen to have a natural explanation. Trances, seizures, prostrations, speaking with tongues, shaking, and quaking, are all recognized now as belonging to the realm of the pathological rather than the theological.

And even mysticism, the last resort of hard-pressed present-day Theists defending supernaturalism, is recognized as a psychical state which can be self-induced even in atheists.

The mystic is simply a person who by meditation and concentration reaches a state of blissful assurance that he is in direct contact with reality, at one with the heart of things. But when the theistic mystic is sure he has been in the very presence of God, it does not prove there is a God, for some of the master mystics of the East, like Gautama Buddha, who make Christian mystics seem like amateurs, had no theistic explanation of their experiences.

As Dr. A. Eustace Haydon, Professor of Comparative Religion at the University of Chicago, has recently pointed out (*The Quest of the Ages*, 1929, pages 192–193):

> "Mystics may be atheists, or pluralists, or theists, or pantheists.
> "The truth the mystic finds is exactly what he has accepted from his social and religious environment. Mystical states are purely subjective. They bring no news from another realm of reality. Their value lies only in giving a warm glow of security to whatever religious world-view the individual may hold."

The supernatural has been driven out of the thunder-riven mountains, the pestilential swamps, the emotional camp-meetings and the cells of the mystics. In every case, phenomena once interpreted by Theists as proof of the existence of a supernatural God, angry or beneficent, have been shown by science to have a perfectly natural explanation.

Very reluctantly has Theism relinquished any ground. It has attempted to erect secondary lines of defence by creating sacred books and churches to which it has attributed infallibility truly miraculous and supernatural. But the science of historical criticism has made short work of these claims to infallibility.

Every position of Theism has been rendered untenable for a modern thinker, but many Theists still remain in those positions, blissfully ignorant of or wilfully blind to the insecurity of the very basis of their faith.

These persistent Theists still pray to "Our Father which art in heaven" and expect to meet departed loved ones in that astronomically impossible place. They still speak of disease and suffering as afflictions sent to try their faith, "for whom the Lord loveth He chasteneth." They still find, either in the emotional outbursts at annual revivals, cleverly produced by itinerant evangelists, or in the self-hypnosis of mystic contemplation, what they continue to call satisfactory evidence of the presence of a personal god.

The great majority of orthodox clergymen have in their libraries only the books they bought while in seminary, largely commentaries and "apologetic" books in defense of the faith. The commentaries are hopelessly out-of-date and the books reassuring one that all is still well are written by men who are not even aware of the real points of attack. Booksellers and librarians throughout the United States agree that clergymen do not buy or borrow the scientific books which the laity are eagerly reading.

Only a few of the clerical exponents of Theism have made themselves sufficiently familiar with modern science to have become aware, in any degree, of the indefensibility of their theological position.

Theism is logically dead, but institutionally still alive, and therefore an obstacle to human progress. It preserves in endowed institutions a bulwark for the support of supernaturalism which can be overthrown only as scientific education acquaints the mass of men with the incompatibility of revealed religion and the discoveries of science.

Humanism seeks to free the human spirit from dependence upon the supernatural because that dependence hinders man's belief in himself upon which Humanism is founded.

Belief in the supernatural is essentially a confession of ignorance of the possibilities of the natural. When one is unaware of his own reserve powers and is unacquainted with certain simple psychological facts, he is apt to interpret as a divine answer to prayer the sudden access of power which tides him over an emergency, and he thinks devoutly, "I never could have done it without God's help."

If man understands his own personality and trains his own powers, he needs no outside God. And if he depends upon an outside God, he by so much hinders the growth of his own personality.

Theism also claims to be interested in man and his improvement but asserts that the improvement of man is best secured by belief in a God. According to theistic teaching, there are certain things man is able to do for himself, but in emergencies man must rely upon God. Man's extremity is held to be God's opportunity.

Humanism would affirm, on the contrary, that man's extremity is his own opportunity. If man habitually leans upon God when the going is hard, and expects God's help when he meets a difficulty, he loses the strength of character which is gained by the extra effort in emergencies.

In such popular proverbs, however, as, "Trust in God, and keep your powder dry," and "God helps those who help themselves," is reflected the common man's practical philosophy, born of experience, which has taught him not to rely solely upon celestial assistance.

And when, at a time of crisis, man does pray and depend on God, and help does come, does that prove that the help came from God? Theism would have us think so. But when such instances are analyzed in the light of all the facts, it becomes evident that no supernatural agency was involved. Either the period of meditation and quiet thinking afforded by the prayer enabled the man to find his own solution of the difficulty, or the help which came was due to the man's own previous efforts, or, as social workers can testify, the help came from some human agency which was at work while the man was praying. Too often, man thanks God for what man has done.

Christian Theism is guilty of having magnified man's "sinfulness" in order, by contrast, to exalt God's goodness. It has taught that since the "Fall of Man" all men have been inherently depraved. To relieve God of the charge that he created man evil, the fiction was taught that the first man was created perfect and stayed so for a while. But ever since, man has been by nature evil.

Consider the effect upon men for many centuries of such scriptural passages as the following verses, especially featured in theistic teaching:

> "Behold, I was shapen in iniquity; and in sin did my mother conceive me."
>
> "The imagination of man's heart is evil from his youth."
>
> "And God saw that the wickedness of man was great in the earth, and that every imagination of the thoughts of his heart was only evil continually."
>
> "How then can man be justified with God? or how can he be clean that is born of a woman? Behold even to the moon, and it shineth not; yea, the stars are not pure in his sight. How much less man, that is a worm? and the son of man, which is a worm?"
>
> "We are all as an unclean thing, and all our righteousnesses are as filthy rags; and we all do fade as a leaf; and our iniquities, like the wind, have taken us away."
>
> "They are all gone aside, they are all together become filthy: there is none that doeth good, no, not one."

Every man has a consciousness of his shortcomings, and theistic theology has taken advantage of that sense of inadequacy, emphasized it, and impressed upon man his utter worthlessness. That overemphasis did its work, and for centuries men have recited such scripture verses in an agony of self-abasement, have begged God's forgiveness, and have sought salvation through grace, as an undeserved favor from a condescending God.

WHAT IS HUMANISM?

Humanism would raise man from such an unworthy position and point out to him that he is not as bad as theologians have taught him to confess. Honest confession is good for the soul, but dishonest confession is not, and every man knows that all men are not gone aside and become filthy. He knows that some men are good most of the time. If he is honest with himself, he knows that he, himself, does many righteous things and that the thoughts of his heart are not evil continually.

Let a man admit his own good qualities to himself: he need not brag about them to others. But he should allow himself credit enough to encourage himself, at least. If there is any saving to be done, and every man knows there is plenty of room in himself for improvement, it is to be done by the man himself with the help of his friends—but not too much help. It is a psychological impossibility for any man or god to "save" another man. A man is never built up in personality and character unless he does it himself. For character is achieved by choosing the right path when one could choose the easier wrong path, and no one can do the choosing but the man himself. Human personality is not only self-perfectible: it is perfectible by no other agency than the self.

Humanism challenges a man to quit leaning on the everlasting arms, and to stop singing:

"Helpless I am and full of guilt."

The time has come for another rebirth of the spirit of man, a new humanistic movement like the Italian Renaissance, but this awakening will be in the realm of religion. John Addington Symonds, in his book on

The Renaissance in Italy, in treating of the revival of learning, wrote:

> "The essence of humanism consisted in a new and vital perception of the dignity of man as a rational being apart from theological determinations, and in the further perception that classic literature alone displayed human nature in the plenitude of intellectual and moral freedom."

What the Renaissance did for literature, a rebirth of the same spirit will do for religion. We need today "a new and vital perception of the dignity of man." Humanism in religion is built upon a recognition of man's essential and native dignity and his infinite possibilities of development. This renaissance in religion will come when man really recognizes his tremendous opportunities and parallel responsibilities.

The modernist wing of Theism maintains that in Theism man's worth is adequately recognized and that Theism is responsible for the growing appreciation of the value of human personality.

It is true that recently there has been a noticeable tendency in all theistic religions to give larger place to human values. Christian preachers have laid increasing stress on the idea of man helping God to make a better world here and now. Salvation by grace still remains in the creeds and hymns, but in the sermons one hears more about salvation by service.

With this change in emphasis has gone a corresponding depreciation in the stock of the supernatural. Miracles were, not such a great while ago, the main reliance of Theists in proving the existence of God. With the advance of science, however, miracles were soon in disrepute, and were not so often featured in theistic sermons. A few of the more progressive Theists began to see that the supernatural itself has no more basis than the Biblical miracles. The wiser and franker of the Theists are admitting the passing of supernaturalism. Dr. Harry Emerson Fosdick recently said:

> "Supernaturalism is an obsolete word and it stands for an obsolete idea. . . . It has become the limbo of the as yet inexplicable, a concept with which we cover our ignorance. The partition of our world into a natural order overlaid by a supernatural order which keeps breaking through is to a well-instructed mind impossible."

Now the growing recognition of the value of human personality has been concomitant with the growing disrepute of the supernatural, and Theism can claim the credit for neither.

Theistic theology has fought bitterly against scientific advance. It has jealously defended the miracles. It was reluctant to part with a single one of them. But in the course of time the church grudgingly admitted that the bizarre miracles of the apocryphal books between the Old and New Testaments were relatively unimportant. Then it relinquished the Old Testament incredibilities. Then, after a struggle to retain all the New Testament miracles at least, it admitted that there might be some doubt about the coin in the fish's mouth and the bodily resurrection of Lazarus. And many Theists who have given up the other miracles still cling to the virgin birth and resurrection of Jesus, save a few in the most advanced circles.

The same story could be told of the gradual recognition of the value of man. In early Christian theology, and even up to a century ago, man was viewed as depraved and as a worm of the dust, but one does not hear that doctrine so much now, save in Fundamentalist pulpits. Instead, some who still call themselves Theists are saying that human personality is "the great central fact of the universe."

Science alone has been responsible for this change in the status of man, and science, be it remarked, was born of the brain of man and not supernaturally revealed.

Knowledge of science has given to man the control of forces which hitherto were supposed to be directed by the supernatural power of God. If God still be God, man has stolen his power. Prometheus has returned to earth and has as yet gone unpunished.

It was therefore inevitable that a very different conception of God should arrive. A Theist who has rejected the supernatural has necessarily redefined the idea of God out of all semblance to its early Christian content.

The God of the early Christians has become hardly more than a figure-head with the Modernists. His supernatural powers have been diminished by the advent of science just as the divine rights and powers of kings have vanished before democracy.

Modernists still maintain that God is king and make due obeisance on state occasions, but he is shorn of his power and is only a symbol. The real power is the Prime Minister, Man.

Modernist Theism is limited monarchy in religion.

Humanism is democracy in religion.

Now it may be that there is as much freedom for the individual in a limited monarchy like Great Britain as there is in a democracy like the United States, but a democracy which supports a king, is, after all, an anomaly.

If we are thoroughgoing in our religious renaissance we shall tarry no longer in the inconsistencies of the limited monarchy of modernist Theism. Rather shall we set up a religious republic of self-governed men.

Democracy is based on the supposition that men are competent to govern themselves and willing to take the trouble to do so. Likewise in a religious democracy the individual must assume more responsibility than in the religions of revelation and authority.

The theistic religions of the past required little more than obedience. A divine revelation claimed by a prophet was formulated by priests into a religion of rites and ceremonies, of codes and creeds. Recite the creed; obey the code; perform the rites or pay someone to do it for you, and all was well. Conform. Believe. Obey. The reward was salvation.

Humanism demands more of the individual than any theistic religion has yet done,—more thinking and planning, more personal responsibility for character-building. There is no magic short-cut to salvation. Self-perfectibility is no easy doctrine. Man is constantly seeking to substitute for it some less arduous procedure. Sugar-coated pills are so much more attractive than strenuous exercises. But spiritual health is not to be had in bottles.

It cannot be purchased. It must be earned.

3 ARE HUMANISTS ATHEISTS?

The charge most frequently brought against Humanists is that they are only a new variety of atheist. The name atheist is used more as an epithet than as an argument and would not deserve an answer were it not for the fact that the main point at issue between Humanists and their opponents is the question of the value of the God-idea.

The question, "Are Humanists atheists?" cannot receive a straight yes-or-no answer because there is no consensus of opinion as to the meaning of the word atheist. The dictionaries are of very little help in the matter. The opprobrium formerly attached to the name is gradually disappearing but traces of it still remain even in works of reference which should be unprejudiced.

The word atheism is used to describe at least four different attitudes toward God, and one cannot answer the question of this chapter without first asking the questioner which sort of atheist he means.

These four kinds of atheism may be classified as agnostic atheism, negative atheism, dogmatic atheism, and moral atheism. And there are shades of difference within each of the four classifications.

An *agnostic atheist* is one who answers the question, "Is there a God?" by saying, "I do not know." He has suspended or withheld judgment. He may not care whether there is a God or not; or he may be intensely interested and constantly searching for evidence. His attitude may be skeptical, critical, scientific, or apathetic. In any event, he is not dogmatic about it, and is ready, or professes to be ready, to hear evidence on either side.

There are those who would deny that such a person is rightly called an atheist at all and would prefer to use the term, agnostic, to describe him. Since there are so many meanings for the word, atheist, it would seem that the word, agnostic, might well be reserved for the person who is undecided on the question of the existence of God.

It must always be borne in mind in dealing with any one of these four classifications of possible atheists that they are all dependent upon the definition of the word, God. An agnostic, for instance, might doubt the existence of one sort of God and yet believe in another. Commonly, however, an agnostic doubts the existence of any kind of God whatsoever.

The *negative atheist* is one who does not believe in God. At first thought it would appear that there is no difference between an agnostic and a negative atheist, for if a man doubts the existence of God, how can he believe in God? The difference is this, that a negative atheist says, "I do not believe in God," while an agnostic says, "I do not know whether there is a God or not." The agnostic is more open-minded: he has not made up his mind on the subject.

On the other side, negative atheism shades off into *dogmatic atheism* which says, "There is no God." The difference between a negative atheist and a dogmatic one is that the former contents himself with observing that for him the evidence is not strong enough to warrant his accepting God as an object of belief.

HUMANISM: A NEW RELIGION

The dogmatic atheist positively asserts that there is no God. On the face of it, that statement is almost as difficult to prove as the assertion that there is a God. Dogmatic atheism goes so far at times as to become actively anti-theistic. Flint, in his book, *Agnosticism,* (1903, sec. 3, p. 53) states that "What is called positive or dogmatic atheism, so far from being the only kind of atheism, is the rarest of all kinds." Possibly, but the group of active, dogmatic, anti-theistic, and even church-hating atheists is certainly growing throughout the world.

The fourth kind of atheism, however, is the sort that is meant when the word is used as an epithet, the *moral atheism* which is opposed not only to the idea of God, but also to all that the idea of God is popularly associated with. Feuerbach, in *The Essence of Christianity,* page 21 of Evans' translation, wrote:

> "He alone is the true atheist to whom the predicates of the Divine Being, for example, love, wisdom and justice, are nothing; not he to whom merely the subject of these predicates is nothing."

The reason why so many people are apparently prejudiced against atheists is because the word connotes to them immorality. In popular usage, an atheist is not merely a person who doesn't believe in God: he is a person who lives a wicked life. Atheism is associated with godlessness, and godlessness is synonymous with immorality. The connection of atheism with wickedness arises from the supposition that a person cannot be good unless he believes in God. Either the fear of God or the love of God is presumed to keep a man from doing evil. God and good are so closely associated in the minds of men that it is very illogically but naturally inferred that he who abjures God necessarily abjures good. In the unreasoning prejudice against atheists a student of folk-psychology easily recognizes a survival of the old belief that he who denies God has sold his soul to the devil.

Now there are immoral atheists, but their number is small, and it is certainly difficult to prove that it is their atheism which makes them immoral. Most atheists one meets are exemplary in their conduct and put to shame many professing Christians.

The question of this chapter, whether or not Humanists are atheists, must be answered in the light of these four classifications.

Certainly Humanists do not belong to the fourth group, those who have lost faith in goodness as well as in God. Their emphasis upon the predicates of the God-idea is pronounced. They are frequently to be found insisting that truth, beauty, and goodness are to be reverenced and sought after with earnestness and patience.

And there are very few, if any, dogmatic atheists among the Humanists. There has been no questionnaire circulated among them to discover how many are dogmatic atheists, but quotations from two American religious Humanists give representative testimonies.

Mr. Alfred W. Hobart, writing in *The New Humanist*, the admirable little magazine published by The Humanist Fellowship of Chicago, stated in the February 1929 issue:

> "Atheism really denotes a dogmatic position, i. e., the denial of God without reservation. I

have yet to meet the Humanist who is an atheist in this sense of the word."

Rev. E. Stanton Hodgin, one of the eighteen ministers contributing to the volume, *Humanist Sermons,* edited by Dr. Curtis Reese, wrote (p. 57):

> "The Humanist is not anti-theistic; to call him an atheist is most unjust and betrays the limitations of the accuser."

Whether the negative atheists number many Humanists among them or not, depends upon the sort of God one means when he says, "I do not believe in God." If one means a supernatural personal deity, most, if not all, Humanists would deny such.

It is among the agnostics that the great majority of Humanists are properly classed. This fact is nothing particularly to be hailed or lamented. There is no virtue or vice today in agnosticism. The rank and file of the Fundamentalist following make no distinction between agnostic and atheist and consider both alike as bound for hell, but in the company of discriminating folk one hears today confessions or avowals of agnosticism so frequently that one reaches the conclusion that a very large proportion, at least, of those who think at all about the existence of God are very doubtful about it.

A significant statement was recently made by a young man in a discussion group at one of the largest New York settlement houses. He said:

> "A lot of us would give up God, for we have come to the point where we doubt his existence, but our early training was such that we are afraid to."

ARE HUMANISTS ATHEISTS?

Orthodoxy would rejoice that the young man's childhood teaching was preserving him from falling into atheism, but Humanism would question the value of the virtue which is retained only through fear of the consequences of abandoning it. Many a person is today hesitating before the difficult hurdle of the effects of early indoctrination. In fact, there are many who fear to admit doubts about the existence of the God of their fathers, even to themselves. They have been told in church and Sunday School that doubt is of the devil and that he who doubts has taken the first step toward atheism.

It is rather pitiful when people who have arrived practically at agnosticism by the use of their reason say, plaintively, "But I can't give up God." Those who cling to an illusion while it is still a reality to them are easily understood; but one who clings to it after grounds for belief in it are gone is admittedly weak in character. He is indulging his emotions at the expense of his intellect.

The problem for such is, how to give up an illusion. And the solution is simply to recognize it as an illusion each time the thought of it arises. Then it will gradually fade, for no one can for long worship devoutly that which he knows at the moment of worship to be an illusion.

There is need for great resolution and strength of character when one decides to seek release from a habit of mind which is popularly supposed to be worthy but which is really subversive to morals. All the devices which appeal to the senses are employed to stupefy the intellect when it comes to the matter of worshipping God. For those who believe, well and good; but for him who seriously doubts the existence of God to go on with the ritual of worship, allowing old associations and subtle appeals to stifle honest agnosticism, is to undermine the very basis of all character.

Some, however, cling to faith in God even when doubting his existence because they have a feeling that while the sort of God they once believed in is impossible for them longer, nevertheless, there may be some sort of revised God, in whom they can honestly believe. But there is a serious question in the minds of many as to whether we have a right to retain the word God when most of its former meaning has been taken from it.

How far exactly may we go in redefining a word? Etymology has plenty of instances where a word has changed its meaning in the process of time until it means almost the opposite of its original sense. But where a word so important as the word God is used by a progressive preacher to mean one thing and is understood by his hearers to mean another, is there not a great danger of misunderstanding and even hypocrisy? And if one must pause every time and define the exact significance of the word, the affair becomes ridiculous. The trouble is further aggravated by the well-known fact that neither preacher nor people has a very definite idea of what the word does mean, except in very orthodox circles. The result is that the meaning of this central word of all theology is blurred and indistinct, which accounts for the muddy thinking in religious matters which is so characteristic of our time.

Dr. A. W. Slaten, in a sermon on *The Idea of God,* (1926), said:

"There is some reason in the contention that we should eliminate the word God from our vocabulary, rather than keep it and give it a new meaning. If that in which we believe is impersonal, unconscious, indifferent force, or energy, why call it by a name that denotes the direct opposite, a personal, conscious being with all the human qualities? Intellectual honesty would seem to demand that we shall not say black when we mean white."

In the last analysis, the attitude of a person toward God, as to whether one is an atheist or not, depends upon his conception of God.

It is impossible and unnecessary here to go into the thousand and one varieties of deity which have been devised by theologians. For our purpose, they can be sufficiently considered under three classifications, the supernatural personal God, the non-supernatural personal God, and the impersonal God.

The *supernatural personal God* has been the God of Judaism and Christianity until very recently. By supernatural we mean miracle working.

Early ideas of God were anthropomorphic. Jehovah was a physical God, not so different from man, but more powerful in every way, a God made in man's own magnified image.

Later ideas of God were more spiritual. In the New Testament, Jehovah became the Heavenly Father, not only a more spiritual deity, but more humane, reflecting man's development.

But God was always supernatural. According to Dr. William N. Clarke, whose book, *The Christian Doctrine of God*, has been the standard theological text-book of American Protestantism, "the supernatural is God himself" (page 341). God had knowledge and power which need take no heed of the natural laws of the universe.

At first, no miracle was too crude for man to believe. But man grew more skeptical of the crasser miracles, until today the English prayer-book has had to omit those which the reasoning mind of modern man absolutely refuses to accept.

And so, gradually, man has had to adjust his idea of God to his increasing knowledge of natural law.

Many devout Theists have abandoned belief in a miracle-working God, but believe in a *non-supernatural personal God*. They hold that there is nothing irreconcilable between religion and science, that God is the author of the laws which man is discovering, and that it was man's ignorance which considered as miracle that which he could not understand.

To them God is personal in the sense that he is a sort of super-personality, with all the good qualities of human personality, magnified to the nth degree, but with none of its limitations. He is completely self-recognizing, self-directing and self-giving, but not physical. He slumbers not nor sleeps. But being personal he can communicate with the soul of man, a lesser personality. The method of communication is a sort of mystic communion in prayer.

But even if it is maintained that the powers of God conform to natural law and that miracles are but the operation of laws as yet beyond the knowledge of man, nevertheless any super-personality, existing apart from man and able to communicate with man, is from the Humanist point of view a supernatural being.

The Humanist cannot agree with the Theist that grounds for belief in such a being lie in the fact that

ARE HUMANISTS ATHEISTS?

there is manifestly a vast area as yet uncharted by the mind of man, nor can he agree with the Theist that the basis for a belief in the existence of a communicating super-personality lies in the conviction of millions of people that prayers are answered. The answers that have come can be explained by natural causes.

Humanists find no evidence that personality exists as a separate entity apart from man.

If one who cannot believe in a supernatural personal deity because he is agnostic concerning the existence of such a being is rightly termed an atheist, then Humanists are atheists. But let it not be inferred that they are therefore without faith in those virtues commonly associated with the name of God and of which God is really the personification.

Many who have practically reached the Humanist position in their thinking are slow to announce themselves as Humanists. There are two reasons for this reluctance.

One is the fear of being misinterpreted as godless and immoral atheists.

The other is the feeling that a gap will be left in their conception of the universe. The idea of God has hitherto served a very useful purpose in explaining the beginning of things.

Before man came there was already life upon the earth, and before that there must have been matter. What developed life from matter, and higher animals from the lower, and man from the higher animals?

There must have been at least a primal energy, a vital impulse, a cosmic urge. Was this not God?

Granted, indeed, that there must have been such

an energy, impulse, or urge, but how can the term God be stretched to cover it?

Some would say, "It was not a personal God, perhaps, but it was God." It is noticeable today that there are many men who are willing to give up the idea of a supernatural God, and even of a personal God, but who are yet searching for justification in believing in some kind of God.

What sort of God could an *impersonal God* be?

There are two varieties of the impersonal God idea, the concept of cosmic consciousness and the concept of cosmic energy.

The phrase "cosmic consciousness" has considerable currency today, and there are a great many people who profess to believe in this idea of God. It is a metaphysical concept and postulates God as pure intelligence or consciousness. Whether or not it is personal is a matter of opinion. It is variously known, as the Absolute, as the Over Soul, as Brahman, and is sometimes identified as the substance of man's own soul. By it man apprehends justice, wisdom, love, and power. It is presumed to be the real source of man's "salvation" and to it is due all the credit for man's nobility.

Such a God obviously cannot be the active agent in the "salvation" of man, and the burden falls on the individual.

The second variety of the strictly impersonal God idea is God considered as cosmic energy, or primal urge. This force, however, is always associated with matter and, except in man, has no conscious purpose, and the name, God, cannot properly be applied to it by any process of reasoning.

The salvation of God by identifying him with the

cosmic energy is a vain compromise of last-ditch Theists. When they sacrifice the personality of God in order to assure his mere existence, they might as well admit defeat.

If one insists, then, on believing in God, he had better cling to the personal God of old-fashioned Theism,—if he intends to be logical at all in his beliefs. But he should also avoid the study of science, unless he can keep science in one part of his mind and religion in another, which requires the maintaining of a very precarious mental equilibrium.

Now, although the cosmic energy is not God, the religious instinct is correct which turns toward it; for religion itself, in a supremely inclusive sense, is the relation of man to this primal urge.

Since man was man he has been conscious of the existence of power in the universe and has been sensitive to its manifestations.

As his consciousness of this energy grew, man sought, childlike, to personify it, to symbolize it, to attribute to it authority over all he could not understand, to clothe it in the spiritual garments of his own ideals, and to worship it.

Elaborate systems of religion with their respective theologies have been evolved for the express and particular purpose of providing a working basis for man in relation to this personified power. But as the mind of man has developed he has become increasingly aware that authority over the power he worshipped lies within himself.

That there is an energy of which man is conscious, on which, by reaching out, man can lay hold, Humanists recognize. But they have rejected the deification of this power. To deny this deification, either in its anthropomorphic or in its spiritual form, is nothing more nor less than to shed an outgrown concept of the imagination of man.

When man gets to the point where he realizes that God was man's own creation for a temporary purpose, he needs God no longer. The idea of God has served its purpose and may be laid aside.

Humanists may differ among themselves concerning the forms and manifestations of the primal energy and its *modus operandi,* but that it exists must be conceded. That this energy operates scientifically through natural laws and not through supernatural means, all intelligent people admit. The Humanist believes that this power cannot be personal, that man himself is the greatest manifestation of this energy, and that it reaches full consciousness only in the personality of man.

Man has begun the study of himself and has discovered that the knowledge and control of energy progress in direct ratio with the development of his personality.

Man can lay hold on this energy only as his mind develops and his knowledge increases of the natural law of the universe. Science, born of the consciousness of man, is the light by which man may perceive how to appropriate this power.

The Humanist does not believe that this energy is a sort of spiritual electricity that vibrates around us in a pure form, to be apprehended mystically, but that it is latent in all forms of material in the universe. There is an energy "sleeping in matter, dreaming in animals, waking in man."

Man himself is a form of this power. There is dawning on him the startling recognition that he is in fact the energy itself taking on consciousness.

He is not the whole of that energy: indeed he is but a small part, but the most valuable part.

He is that part which has come to consciousness, so far as he *has* done so. The other forms of energy outside himself he must lay hold on and appropriate for his own use. The transfer of energy to serve the ends of higher personality is the problem of civilization. Science deals specifically with the study of natural law to this end.

Man discovers in himself parts of the primal energy which have not yet come to consciousness. His body is matter which inherits the legacy of the period when the primal energy was not conscious. His subconscious is a vast storehouse of inherited tendencies which are available for his conscious use. His brain, so he has lately discovered, has virgin areas in which may be developed new powers as yet unguessed.

In the proportion as he becomes more conscious and self-recognizing, he promotes the development of the primal energy itself. In him the struggle of life proceeds, vacillating between periods of unconsciousness and consciousness. He is the crucial point of the higher evolution.

Man has become conscious enough to direct to some extent the progress of the eternal energy within himself and outside himself.

Man's value is therefore inestimable, priceless. As he develops his personality he partakes in creative evolution.

Humanistic religion deals with the relation of the individual to this power or energy resident in himself and in the universe and concerns itself particularly with the growth of the higher consciousness or the personality of man, socially and individually, believing that man is potentially able by his own efforts to attain to the complete and perfected personality to which all religion aspires.

4 THE ANCESTRY OF HUMANISM

In the light of recent humanistic progress, it is possible to look back over the past and examine with fresh interest the men and movements that heralded Humanism. There is ample material for a History of Humanism, or, if it be objected that Humanism is too young to have a history, a story of The Rise of Humanism.

Our concern in this chapter, however, is a very brief and cursory outline of the forerunners of Humanism. Many strains combined to produce the modern humanistic temper. To trace each of them from its origin is impossible here: we shall simply indicate the most significant.

The main line of development starts from the Greek Humanists of the fifth century before Christ. Then it is not to be seen, save for isolated and sporadic appearances, until it is found nearly nineteen centuries later in what is called the Rebirth, or Renaissance, in the fourteenth, fifteenth, and sixteenth centuries. The Encyclopedists of the eighteenth century and the Positivists of the nineteenth are in the line, or closely parallel, and the twentieth century has seen the sudden branching out of Humanism into every department of life.

Before we trace the main line, however, it is necessary to recognize another genealogy, which, in the far east, has produced another Humanism of which the west is just becoming conscious.

HUMANISM: A NEW RELIGION

To the average westerner, a Christian of Europe or America, for instance, religion without God is almost inconceivable. But in the east, religion without God is no novelty. Buddhism, Hinduism, Jainism, Taoism, and Confucianism, have, in certain sections and at certain times, been godless religions.

Buddha, Lao-Tsze, and Confucius were atheists, or at least agnostics; and Mahavira the Jain and Kapila the brilliant founder of the Sankhya doctrine of Hinduism were out and out atheists. The followers of these men later made theistic additions and interpretations, but the original and pure doctrines of these mighty religions were non-theistic.

In Buddha's Eight-fold Path and Four Noble Truths which sum up his whole religious teaching there is no mention of any deity.

Kapila's Sankhya doctrine had a direct influence on Alexandrian gnosticism which for a time so harassed the leaders of early Christianity and which was finally rejected as heretical. In gnosticism, God was It rather than He, and was so transcendent as to be practically non-existent.

Mahavira rejected and denounced the idea of a Creator God or a Heavenly Helper of men and uttered the humanistic advice:

> "Man! Thou art thy own friend! Why wishest thou for a friend beyond thyself?" (*Sacred Books of the East*, 22: 33.)

The "Tao," the central doctrine of Lao-Tsze, can best be translated "reason," and the scriptures, the *Tao-Teh-King*, is simply "The Book of the Path of Virtue."

Prayer, worship, immortality, and belief in a per-

THE ANCESTRY OF HUMANISM

sonal God were, for Confucius, unimportant in religion. He did not deny the existence of supernatural beings, but urged his followers not to depend on them and to practice self-culture.

The great humanistic developments of culture in Greece of the fifth century B.C. and of Europe of the Renaissance period flowered at times of material prosperity. China does not, at present, afford a similar favorable economic environment, owing to unsettled conditions.

It is probable that the next great humanistic culture will develop in America. It is significant that just as the revival of interest in classical Greek studies in Europe occurred at the Renaissance, there is in America a similar if not altogether parallel revival of interest in the religions of the east. Americans are avidly perusing books on eastern religions. The old Vedic literature, which has hitherto been almost unknown here, is lately attracting much attention. Brahmanic and Buddhistic religion is reflected in a dozen cults already. Many persons who have left the Christian fold are discovering that some "heathen" prophets were decidedly humanistic and said many things which Christians have yet to learn.

The impact of the Humanism of the east upon western thought which has already evolved a Humanism of its own is likely to have important results in the next few decades. It is significant that there is a magazine published in Bangalore called *The Humanist* and one published in Chicago, *The New Humanist,* by students in a Christian theological seminary. It may be that east and west will yet find their meeting-place in the religion of Humanism.

It is from the Greek Humanists, however, and

HUMANISM: A NEW RELIGION

through the Renaissance, that modern western Humanism derives.

In the sixth century B. C. lived two Greek philosophers, Thales of Miletus and Xenophanes of Colophon, both of whom were pantheists. Neither can be called a Humanist, yet they prepared the way for the new type of philosophy, the study of man himself rather than the gods or the cosmos, which flourished in the following century.

Thales was the first great Greek philosopher and sought through reason rather than revelation to discover some principle which would explain the universe. He decided that it was water and sought to prove that all things came from water and would ultimately return to their source. The fact that he was mistaken in the principle is not so important as that he believed that man could explain the universe by the use of his reason. He is credited with two other teachings which connect him with Humanism; one of which was the Golden Rule of treating others as one would like to be treated, and the other, the maxim, "Know thyself."

Socrates is usually referred to as the author of these famous two words, but in Socrates' day the maxim was already contained in the inscription over the temple of the Delphic god. Quite likely, Thales too was quoting, but he antedated Socrates by over a century.

As for the Golden Rule, it is impossible to determine its first promulgation, as it is found in practically every great religious literature, in at least seven before Christianity. It ought to be called The Great Humanist Commandment, and if a world religion ever arrives, this maxim will be central in it.

THE ANCESTRY OF HUMANISM

If Thales is its author, Humanists hail him as a kindred spirit. It should be noted that the Golden Rule is quite non-theistic. Those who accept it as a sufficient guide for conduct are good Humanists.

Xenophanes, although his estimate of the smallness of man rules him out of the class of even near-humanists, did give utterance to an idea frequently brought into arguments against Theism. He pointed out that the gods of any nation were pictured as having the physical characteristics of the men of that nation. Ethiopian gods were black with flat noses: Thracian gods were blond. Oxen, lions, and horses, if they made gods, would make them in their own image and likeness. So Xenophanes refused to recognize the gods of his time and preferred to reserve the name of God for the principle of unity in the universe.

When Anaxagoras left Ionia for Athens early in the fifth century B. C., he took with him a precious cargo. To him goes the honor for the introduction of a developed philosophy and a real science. To Athenians holding the view that the sun was a deity, he boldly proclaimed that it was a fiery mass of matter larger than the Peloponnesus, and that the other celestial bodies had also been cast forth into the ether from the revolving world. With remarkable forecasting of later astronomy he said that the moon had mountains and plains and valleys like the earth. The central principle he defined as mind operating on matter, and he taught that matter was composed of very small seeds, a theory of matter anticipating the atomic.

Such atheistic views met with opposition and persecution. He has been called "the first freethinker historically known to have been legally prosecuted and condemned for his freethought." (J. M. Robertson, *Short History of Free Thought*, I, 152.)

But Anaxagoras had an able defender, his own pupil, Pericles, for whom this whole period of Greek history has been named. Pericles procured for his master a commutation of the death sentence to life banishment. The Athenians soon found that the departure of the heretic did not mean that his heresy had also been eliminated.

The rationalist attitude in religion which Pericles championed made him unpopular, but he succeeded in becoming the chief statesman of Greece and maintaining that position for a generation. In the course of his brilliant career he put into the very character of the Greeks the principles which Anaxagoras had advocated and which he himself developed further in company with a remarkable group of humanistic friends. Those principles were democracy, freedom of thought, and the exposure of superstitions. He encouraged the arts with the result that a culture developed which has yet to be matched.

Within ten years of the birth of Pericles, Herodotus, Euripides, and Protagoras had been born; and a little later came a second generation of Humanists, Socrates, Democritus, and Thucydides, who all grew to manhood before the death of Pericles.

Herodotus has been called both "the father of history" and "the father of Humanists." He does not deserve the latter title as much as does Anaxagoras, but with the other contemporaries of Pericles he did contribute greatly to the discovery of man which marks the period.

Euripides the dramatist was a follower of Anaxagoras and a friend of Protagoras and Socrates. Gilbert Murray says of him:

> "He can safely be called the poet of the Sophistic movement, . . . (which) was, on the whole, agnostic. . . . It urged men to look for evidence, to use their understanding and their common sense. . . . The thought of Euripides is in many ways extraordinarily advanced, not only for his own age but for any succeeding age." (*Encyc. Religion and Ethics,* V, 588–91.)

In Protagoras we discover a real Humanist. His famous sentence, "Man is the measure of all things," was the Emancipation Proclamation of the human race. Concerning the gods, he was openly agnostic, and said:

> "Of the gods I cannot say whether they exist or not, nor of what nature they are. For there are many obstacles to inquiry, especially the obscurity of the problem and the shortness of life." (*Diog. Laert.* ix, 51.)

Several ancient authorities assert that Protagoras was condemned and all available copies of his treatise on the gods burned publicly and that he was drowned at sea as he fled to save his life. Most of his writings are lost forever, save fragments and quotations. It is interesting that the work containing his most famous sentence was popularly known as The Truth.

F. A. Lange, in his *History of Materialism,* says of him:

> "Protagoras marks a great and decisive turning point in the history of Greek philosophy. He is the first who started, not from the object —from external nature, but from the subject— from the spiritual nature of man."

His message to his fellows, to use his own words, was "to make men good citizens."

Socrates was less a Humanist than was Protagoras. He recognized the gods, but he placed the chief emphasis on the development of the moral nature of man.

Democritus ranks among the profoundest minds of antiquity and must be considered one of the outstanding Humanists. His views were purely nontheistic, for he discovered no providence nor intelligent purpose in the universe. He developed the atomic theory, which, up to our own day, contributed so much to the understanding of the universe. That universe was for him quite mechanical, but his system cannot be identified with the fortuitous mechanism of today. He did not believe in the immortality of the soul, but did believe in the cultivation of the soul. He urged tranquillity, temperance in all things, and good humor. He has been compared favorably with Aristotle and Plato. Unfortunately, of his more than seventy works, only a scanty few survive, but he made an impression on his contemporaries not only by his great learning but also by his upright private life and happy disposition. The "Laughing Philosopher" lived the Humanism he taught.

The historian Thucydides was less credulous and superstitious than Herodotus, more scientific in his approach to history. As a disciple of Anaxagoras he had learned the value of rationalism, and his outlook on life and his interpretation of history were therefore characterized by the humanistic temper.

These eight men, Anaxagoras, Pericles, Herodotus, Euripides, Protagoras, Socrates, Democritus, and

THE ANCESTRY OF HUMANISM

Thucydides, represent the cream of fifth century Greek Humanism. Into all fields of human thought, particularly philosophy, they penetrated with a new spirit and created a culture to which we may still turn in admiration.

Between the fifth century B. C. and the fourteenth A. D. there was no humanistic period. There were lonely individuals who approached Humanism, but who were more negative than positive. Carneades, the Greek philosopher of the second century B. C., was a skeptic and an agnostic. Julius Cæsar, high priest of Roman religion though he was, nevertheless exhibited many of the marks of the freethinker. And the satirist Lucian of the second Christian century very pointedly made fun of theistic ideas.

In the twelfth century two Arab philosophers, Avempace and Averroes had marked inclinations toward Humanism, and two Christian bishops, Hildebert of Lavardin and John of Salisbury were forerunners of the literary Humanism of the Renaissance.

The philosophical Humanism of the Greeks was a protest against absolutism, and the literary Humanism of the Renaissance contended against scholasticism. The intellectualism of the scholastic period was completely subservient to ecclesiastical authority, an authority which had for centuries cramped the human spirit by insisting on the doctrine of the Fall of Man and salvation attainable only by the grace of God.

Of the Renaissance Humanism, John Addington Symonds says (*Renaissance in Italy:* The Revival of Learning. 1883. p. 72):

HUMANISM: A NEW RELIGION

> "It was partly a reaction against ecclesiastical despotism, partly an attempt to find the point of unity for all that had been thought and done by man, within the mind restored to consciousness of its own sovereign faculty. Hence the single-hearted devotion to the literature of Greece and Rome that marks the whole Renaissance era. Hence the watchword of that age, the *Litterae Humaniores*. Hence the passion for antiquity, possessing thoughtful men, and substituting a new authority for the traditions of the Church. Hence the so-called Paganism of centuries bent upon absorbing and assimilating a spirit no less life-giving from their point of view than Christianity itself. Hence the persistent effort of philosophers to find the meeting-point of two divergent inspirations. Hence, too, the ultimate antagonism between the Humanists, or professors of the new wisdom, and those uncompromising Christians who, like St. Paul, preferred to remain fools for Christ's sake."

In the thirteenth century education awoke in Europe, but the newly founded universities were swamped by the scholasticism of the day. Dante, who lived in both centuries, bridges the chasm between the thirteenth and the fourteenth.

Petrarch was the first child of the Rebirth, "the first modern man." With him must be coupled his friend Boccaccio and Boccaccio's younger friend Salutato. These names stand out as the Humanists of the fourteenth century.

Petrarch was less combative than Boccaccio, but more of a rationalist. The author of the Decameron was a product of his time and a leader of its revolt as well. His trenchant pen caricatured the immoral

THE ANCESTRY OF HUMANISM

clericalism of the day and also revealed the wild excesses of the joy in the new freedom of man.

Salutato was a scholar and a collector of manuscripts, and both by his writings and his personal influence did much to stimulate the love of classical learning.

The leading Italian Humanists of the fifteenth century were Niccolo Niccoli, Vittorino da Feltre, Poggio Bracciolini, Parentucelli, Filelfo, Piccolomini, Lorenzo Valla, Laetus, Poliziano, and Pico della Mirandola.

Parentucelli was Pope Nicholas V and Piccolomini was Pope Pius II.

Some of these men were Humanists only in the sense of being passionately devoted to the new learning, and were interested more in collecting manuscripts of the Greek and Latin classics than in contributing to the thought of their time.

But Vittorino da Feltre and Lorenzo Valla deserve special mention for their constructive activities. The former was a pioneer educator and anticipated some of the methods of Pestalozzi by three and a half centuries. Valla was a brilliant scholar, probably the greatest of the century if not of the whole Renaissance.

Valla not only translated Homer, Herodotus and Thucydides into Latin, but his comparison of the Vulgate of the New Testament with the original Greek revealed him as one of the earliest higher critics. He discovered several forgeries in accepted documents of the church and was immediately unpopular with the ecclesiastical authorities, barely escaping the Inquisition. He was a rationalist and somewhat of a freethinker and did not hesitate to attack the church. Dr. Preserved Smith, in his volume on Erasmus, who intensely admired Valla, says (p. 15)

> "Valla was an incarnation of the intellectual Renaissance, a critic and iconoclast of the caliber almost of Voltaire, unparalleled as yet in modern Europe for the daring, acumen, force, irreverence, and brilliancy of his attacks on religion. True, Valla called himself a Christian, and probably without hypocrisy, but his ideal was of a purely moral, humanitarian religion, unhampered either by creed or by ritual."

Valla's successor as a Biblical critic was Pomponazzi, another skeptic and freethinker who yet remained within the church. Pomponazzi was bold enough to attempt to explain the miracles on a rational basis and also to make an assertion which is still debated in our day, namely that an ethical life is possible without a belief in immortality.

Pomponazzi introduces us to the sixteenth century, for he did not die until it had reached its first quarter. He is the last great Italian Humanist, unless one reckons Machiavelli one. This statesman considered the church evil and held that its doctrine of finding the abject and humble men the most desirable citizens really abandoned the state to the rule of scoundrelly rascals. He nevertheless argued for religion in the state, although he was an unbeliever, because he considered it desirable politically.

The sixteenth century finds the Humanist movement spreading outside Italy. In England, John Colet and Sir Thomas More; in Spain, Juan Luis Vives; in France, François Rabelais and Pierre de la Ramée;

in Germany, Konrad Mut (Mutianus Rufus), Ulrich von Hutten, and Philip Melanchthon held high the torch of the new freedom.

But "the prince of Humanists" was Desiderius Erasmus of Rotterdam and all western Europe. He was an independent and original scholar of great ability and profound learning who wrote many books in a brilliant and interesting style. His books were "humanized" outlines of learning for the people, and his letters were clever compositions of rare persuasiveness for men of high station. He was a master of the personal letter and his voluminous correspondence with more than five hundred men, many of them leaders of the day, did more to extend the humanistic movement than has commonly been recognized. To read his life and letters is to get a conception of the spirit, the extent, and the influence of Renaissance Humanism not to be so well attained in any other way.

No knight ever jousted more stoutly, enthusiastically, and cleverly against foes in armor than did Erasmus with his pen against superstition and ignorance and ecclesiastical pretensions. It has been often repeated that he "laid the egg that Luther hatched," yet he was not a Protestant reformer in the usual sense of the word. He always remained in the Catholic church, although a thorn in its side.

With Erasmus the Renaissance reached its climax. "Letters" had been "revived." There was little more that man could learn from the past, even the humanistic past. Humanism had made the modern age possible. It henceforth became the task of the men of humanistic temper to consider the present and look to the future.

While Erasmus was a young man in his twenties, another man in his forties discovered America, and before Erasmus died in 1536 the world was very much larger than it had been when he was born in 1469.

The sixteenth and seventeenth centuries enlarged the world of knowledge not only geographically but in many other ways. The Renaissance had started men thinking. Sciences came into being and, under the guise of "Natural Philosophy," fought their way to recognition in the universities.

The mass of new knowledge was of great interest to all men and there arose a demand for books containing it. From that demand the modern type of encyclopedia arose. There had been encyclopedias of a sort in the times of the Greeks and Romans and many since. Every new accession of knowledge brought new encyclopedias. They were arranged in what seem to us strange ways: the subject-groupings were according to philosophical theories, or chronologically, or by various bizarre schemes. The alphabetical or dictionary encyclopedias appear first about the middle of the seventeenth century. In other words, general knowledge was made more accessible. The process of making knowledge more available has gone on until the latest Britannica is advertised as a "humanized" encyclopedia.

Various experiments in the new type of compendiums of knowledge appeared in the late seventeenth and early eighteenth centuries. Gradually they became more comprehensive. In 1728 appeared Ephraim Chambers' *Cyclopedia,* comprehensive, scholarly and introducing the system of cross-references, the first, really, of the admirable English encyclopedias.

Chambers' *Cyclopedia* was translated into French by John Mills and revised and greatly enlarged by Diderot and published in 28 volumes from 1751 to 1772. Diderot had the help of D'Alembert, Rousseau, Voltaire, Montesquieu, and many other brilliant scholars, who were consequently called "The Encyclopedists."

The reason for including these men among the Humanists is plain when we note that they seized the opportunity to insert in their great encyclopedia their own rationalistic views, often materialistic and radically opposed to the current religion. Diderot and his companions incurred the opposition and persecution of theologians and other censors, but succeeded in completing the great work. Its influence in liberating thought was felt not only in France, but in Germany.

Goethe, whose realistic writings, with their emphasis on the correlation of thought and action, must be reckoned among the great contributions to the trend toward Humanism, was keenly interested in the work of the Encyclopedists, was especially influenced by Diderot and Rousseau, and translated into German an essay on painting from the Encyclopedia.

Sporadic manifestations of the humanistic spirit were evident in many men and movements during the eighteenth and nineteenth centuries. It is possible here to chronicle only conspicuous ones.

In the early eighteenth, Alexander Pope gave utterance to a couplet which has since been often quoted by Humanists:

"Know then thyself, presume not God to scan;
 The proper study of mankind is man."

HUMANISM: A NEW RELIGION

In the middle eighteenth, a movement known as Humanitarian appeared as a theological protest against the doctrines of the trinity and the deity of Jesus. It developed into the Unitarian churches of England.

In the middle nineteenth, the same name, Humanitarians, was applied to the followers of Pierre Leroux, a French radical, who continued the propaganda work of Diderot's Encyclopedists, and taught that the perfection of man might be attained without divine assistance.

The nineteenth century movement most frequently associated with the name Humanism, however, is Comte's positivism. The word positive is not to be taken in the sense of the opposite of negative, but as meaning certain, assured, scientific.

Comte's central doctrine was the Law of the Three Stages, the theological, the metaphysical, and the positive. Through these intellectual periods the individual and the race must pass. The origin and control of all phenomena is explained in the theological stage as due to a supernatural God, and in the metaphysical stage, to abstract forces. In the positive stage, theology and metaphysics are reckoned futile and harmful, and only the certain or positive facts and their relations, ("the discovery of the laws of phenomena") are considered. All the real intellectual and emotional needs of men are included in a new doctrine of society, based on positivistic principles.

This philosophy of positivism was organized by Comte into a religion, *la réligion de l'humanité,* an iron-clad system in which every detail and possible development was prescribed and anticipated by the founder, and which reflected only too accurately his idiosyncrasies.

Auguste Comte was an unusual man. Had he possessed mental balance and a better practical knowledge of the human nature he talked about so much, he might have been a great man. As it was, he was a peculiar combination of intellectual acumen and of absurd notions merging into insanity. He had, nevertheless, a great many personal friends and admirers who furnished him financial support, among whom was John Stuart Mill. His best known work, a six volume treatise on positivism, was translated into English by Harriet Martineau in 1853, eight years after she had left Unitarianism for agnosticism.

When Comte was but a young man, he met and became for a time the disciple of the French social theorist, Saint-Simon. Although he left Saint-Simon, the influence remained with him, for he had learned the theory of his teacher, "to study the progress of the human mind in order to work thenceforth for the perfecting of civilization." Comte's religion of humanity was in some aspects akin to Saint-Simon's humanistic social doctrines.

The tragedy of Comte's Humanism was his failure to allow room for change and development in his movement. His egotism prevented him from seeing that no one man can draw rigid plans for a movement so wide-spreading and all embracing as the one he contemplated. Both Comte's knowledge and his experience were too limited, and his philosophical system too much clogged with abstractions carried out to minute details.

There are still a few congregations surviving in

England and South America, meticulously preserving the traditions established by their leader as to doctrine, form of organization, and form of worship. Even their temples are built according to plans drawn by Comte.

Theology and metaphysics were taboo in the Positivist cult, but, in other ways, there are startling resemblances to Roman Catholicism. In their temples, a statue of Comte stands at the entrance end and a statue of the Sistine Madonna at the chancel end. Humanity is really worshipped in the person of the virgin.

Comte's religion was just that, the worship of humanity. Herein it differed greatly from the religion of Humanism now evolving in America, which is not interested in the worship of humanity nor in any worship at all, but seeks, rather, the improvement of humanity.

Current criticism of modern Humanism constantly confuses it with positivism. Against that mistaken assumption, Edwin H. Wilson, an authority on positivism, protests vigorously in an illuminating article, Positivism and Humanism, in the January 1930 issue of the *Open Court* magazine:

> "The two movements are so unlike that the effort to use Positivism as a shibboleth for Humanism is not justified on the grounds either of content or of form. To be sure, both movements might be said to be religions of life, based upon the things of this life. But their respective ideas of what true religion is, what life values are most worthful, what constitutes evidence, and how the religion of humanity is best to be stated and propagated, are so unlike that the movements

are altogether different plants producing different fruits. . . .

"Positivism is a hybrid developed in the stuffy hothouse climate of one man's study. It bears the limitations of that man's personal foibles, we might fairly say abnormalities. It bears, moreover, the limitations of his century. The time was not yet ripe for such a synthesis. . . . Humanism has a grasp of the problems of the inner life not within Comte's range of experience. . . . We must bear in mind that Humanism has tools which Comte did not have to help him in his work. The results of half a century's research in the social science are now available. It has an immense body of new facts and hence a sounder orientation. It has at its disposal a developed method of research which controls the subjective limitations which handicapped Comte's system of thought."

While Comte was imbibing the social philosophy of Saint-Simon in Paris, a religious movement came to birth in America which was destined to prove the immediate parent of twentieth century Humanism.

In 1819, at the ordination of Jared Sparks in Baltimore, William Ellery Channing preached a sermon defining and defending the position of the radical wing of Congregationalism known as Unitarianism.

On May 25, 1825, a group of young men in Boston founded the American Unitarian Association on the very day, by coincidence, that in London the British and Foreign Unitarian Association was founded. For many decades liberal tendencies in religion had been quietly growing in both countries. While the Humanitarian forerunners of English Unitarianism were establishing themselves, in the middle of the eighteenth century, Jonathan Mayhew, the first and lonely American Unitarian, was preaching his heresies in Boston.

Unitarianism was liberal Christian theism, but it was from the beginning strongly humanistic in its trend. Any reform calculated to improve the conditions of human living was sure of Unitarian support; indeed, most American reforms of the last century have been fathered or mothered by representatives of that denomination. And its theology has grown steadily more humanistic. Members have been welcome in its fellowship who questioned not only supernaturalism but also the existence of a personal God. Many openly referred to God as a cosmic force.

It is not to be wondered at but looked upon as a natural development that some forty Unitarian ministers have lately been reckoned as Humanists of various degrees, while many more are evidently contemplating the step.

The "dean" of American Humanists, Dr. John H. Dietrich, Minister of the First Unitarian Church of Minneapolis, who has preached the new doctrine for fifteen years, stressed the point that Unitarianism is natural soil for Humanism in a sermon preached five years ago, which is here quoted as of historic significance. The address was delivered before the First Unitarian Society of Minneapolis, Sunday morning, June 8, 1925, and was entitled, *"Humanism, the Next Step in Religion."*

> "Unitarianism offered opportunity for the enunciation of Humanism by virtue of its underlying principle of spiritual freedom, by its insistence upon intellectual integrity rather than intellectual uniformity, by its offer of religious fellowship to every one of moral purpose without regard to his theological beliefs. But this

is not the important thing. The real reason why Unitarianism was the natural soil for the growth of Humanism is the fact that Unitarianism was a revolt against orthodox Christianity in the interest of the worth and dignity of human nature and the sanctity of human life. The real origin of Unitarianism is to be found in the revolutionary interpretation of human nature which was taught by Channing and his colleagues. . . .

"Now it is only a step from this thought to another which forms the basis of Humanism, that man not only is of worth, but of supreme worth, namely, that he is an end and not a means. In other words, Humanism is merely an expansion and a more rigorous application of the fundamental principle of Unitarianism. Indeed, Channing announced this logical conclusion, but it has not been fully preached by the majority of Unitarians."

It is true that William Ellery Channing sowed the seeds of Humanism in Unitarianism, but it is also true that Channing lived and died a theist, and that it was some time before the seeds bore fruit.

Just a century elapsed between Channing's Baltimore sermon which defined Unitarianism and three addresses which brought Humanism to the attention of theologians.

It was in May, 1919, that Dr. Dietrich spoke in Chicago at the Western Unitarian Conference on "The Outlook for Religion" and in October of the same year that he addressed the Unitarian General Conference at Detroit on "The Faith That Is in Us." The next summer Dr. Curtis W. Reese, secretary of the Western Unitarian Conference, who had been preaching what he called the religion of democracy, gave an address at Harvard University to a summer school gathering of Unitarian ministers in which he took the Humanist position.

These three addresses precipitated a controversy in the Unitarian denomination which is still being waged with increasing earnestness on both sides, and which has also spread to the Universalists. The growth of humanism has not been confined to these two denominations, but is spreading in the liberal wings of the Quakers and other groups.

In January of this year, five university professors sent several thousand letters throughout the country, calling men to modernize Christianity, but urging such radical changes that little of classical Christianity is left. The resultant religion is openly humanistic, as the following passage indicates:

> "I am proposing that we substitute the inspiring power of the vision of an ideal humanity for fear of hell and hope of heaven as a driving power in the life of men; and that God within—the unifying element which drives men to unity in a brotherly world—replace a medieval, imperial deity who makes irrational demands on his human subjects and savagely punishes or extravagantly rewards those who anger or please him; who looks upon this world and its happiness as immaterial or evil, centering all interest on a supposed life after death."

(The letter was sent by Dr. Jesse H. Holmes of Swarthmore College and was also signed by Dean Roscoe Pound of the Harvard Law School, Professor J. Russell Smith of Columbia, Professor Thomas A. Jenkins of the University of Chicago, and Professor Albert T. Mills of James Milliken University.)

THE ANCESTRY OF HUMANISM

One reason for the great public interest in humanism in religion is the growth of the humanistic point-of-view in other departments of life, well-stated by Dr. Dietrich in the following paragraph:

"Today the humanistic spirit is sweeping the whole field of thought and endeavor. Modern *philosophy* has placed human nature at the center of the knowledge process and defines values in terms of the relation of things to human living. Those things are of value which foster and contribute to human welfare, while those which impoverish and detract from human life are bad. This is what we mean by humanistic philosophy. *Science* also has become predominantly humanistic in that it investigates cosmic processes for the purpose of using and controlling them for human ends. In *education* the trend has become entirely humanistic, and we educate our children because we want them to acquire such knowledge as will help them make life worth while. Herbert Spencer said, 'The function of education is to prepare us for complete living,' which is a purely humanistic definition of education and has become the prevailing motive among modern educators. And there are some of us who feel that *religion* should also thus become humanistic by grounding spirituality, if I may use that term, in human living rather than in some supernatural existence, by interpreting the good life in terms of human values, and by directing man's religious aspirations toward the enhancement of human life."

Dr. Dietrich might well have included music, art, and literature as invaded by the humanistic trend.

Literature, indeed, is having a humanistic revival of its own, so generally recognized that to many persons Humanism does not mean a religion, but a modern literary renaissance.

This literary, or academic Humanism will be discussed in Chapter Nine, under the heading, Is Humanism a Religion?

5 WAS JESUS A HUMANIST?

In the foregoing chapter the name of Jesus was purposely omitted from the list of those who were forerunners of Humanism because the question of his inclusion as a Humanist is a debatable one and deserves separate consideration.

Before we take up the question, Was Jesus a Humanist? we need to ask the related questions, Are Humanists Christians? and Was Jesus a Christian?

Some among the Humanists would consider themselves Christians, taking the word in a broad sense, but others would refuse the appellation. It depends upon whether one features the obvious historical fact that Humanism has grown out of Christianity or the equally patent fact that it has outgrown Christianity. There are advantages in preserving the historical connection and there are decided disadvantages in so doing.

Inasmuch, however, as there are Humanists in growing numbers who have come from Jewish, Muhammadan, Confucian, Buddhist, and Hindu backgrounds, and who agree in all essentials with the Humanism which is of Christian origin, it is evident that the question whether Humanists are Christians or not will gradually lose importance, although it may be for a few years a live issue in Christian countries.

Unitarians of the theist wing would certainly not call the Humanists Christians.

But other Protestant denominations do not call Unitarians Christians. In fact, Unitarians are not included in the Federal Council of Churches of Christ in America, the great central body of American Protestantism.

And Protestants are not reckoned Christians by the Roman Catholics.

And it is doubtful whether a Roman Catholic of today would be recognized as a fellow Christian by a member of one of the early Christian churches founded by Paul.

And still more doubtful is it if one of Paul's converts, or Paul himself, would have been thought by the Carpenter of Nazareth to be one of his disciples.

The great disparity in points of view and in emphasis between the teachings of Paul and those of Jesus has been denied by those interested in preserving the tradition of the continuity of Christian doctrine from Jesus to the present time, but one has only to compare the Epistle to the Romans with the Sermon on the Mount.

If Paul was a Christian, Jesus was not.

That is, if the gospels are true records. Modern Christian scholarship insists that all parts are not equally reliable.

If the documents are questionable, we do not know whether Jesus was like modern Christians or not. He may have been more like the Humanists.

But if the gospel records are reasonably accurate, and if we make allowance for interpolations and misinterpretations by his biographers, it may be shown that Jesus was a Theist, but imbued with the spirit of Humanism and well on the way to it. Perhaps Jesus was as much of a Humanist as anyone in his environ-

WAS JESUS A HUMANIST?

ment could have been. But Paul was not, and Christian theology has historically followed Paul rather than Jesus.

Taking Christ to represent the theological figure created by Paul and later theologians, and Jesus as the historical person, it might be said with considerable truth that Christ was more of a Theist and Jesus more of a Humanist.

To make the point more obvious, recall the definition of Humanism. Did Jesus believe in "the supreme value and self-perfectibility of human personality"?

There are many passages to indicate that he did. There are none to indicate that Paul did, and we have an abundance of Paul's own letters, but none of Jesus', only second- or third-hand reports of his conversations. Perhaps his more humanistic sayings were omitted by those who did not understand them or who left them out as too utterly heretical. We have to remember that all his chroniclers were Theists and that they would naturally see him and hear him through a cloud of theistic theology. Try as they might to present his teachings accurately, they were so convinced of his goodness that they must needs invest him with opinions which to their minds were held by all good men, with the result that even his humanistic utterances are probably overlaid with a plating of Theism.

The remarkable power of Jesus and the equally remarkable spread of Christianity after his death have commonly been accounted for by the statement that he was God himself come down to earth for a brief stay. Other religious leaders in other lands have been similarly deified.

A more satisfactory scientific explanation than

deity is surely to be sought. When his followers deified him, they were simply exhibiting the poverty of their vocabulary. Deification was their only superlative. In their immature science, hardly worthy of the name, supernaturalism was accepted as a fact.

We have too long explained Jesus theologically. The time has come to study him psychologically.

The humanist way of explaining his influence is by recognizing it as due to his remarkably developed personality. His self-recognition had proceeded to a point where it provoked exclamations at his air of assurance and authority. His self-direction was so marked that legends grew up that he could go where he willed, on the surface of the waves or through closed doors. His self-giving so impressed the recipients of the outflow of his sympathy that they felt that virtue emanated from his very clothing. His entire personality gave to all who came in contact with him the impression of great reserve power. The impact of his friendly and puissant nature upon those around him, particularly his evident belief in their possibilities, thrilled and roused them to live better lives. It is no wonder that they thought there was something supernatural about him. And after he died the stories of his miracles grew and multiplied.

His followers were convinced that such a personality must persist beyond the grave, and they soon had him pictured as risen from the dead and seated at the right hand of Jehovah.

The central belief of Jesus' life was that God was his Heavenly Father and had acknowledged him as His son. It was Theism, to be sure, but a very personal sort of Theism. His God was the Jewish God of his forefathers, but he felt in a particularly inti-

WAS JESUS A HUMANIST?

mate relation to that God. The term Father was the most intimate word he could use to express that relation. The fact that he evidently expected to go to that Father at death would seem to indicate that he conceived him as distinct from himself, but he also seemed to feel in very close relation to that Father during his earthly life. It was, in fact, a sort of humanized Theism, a warm personalized Theism which he held.

Of the power resident in himself he was conscious. His early recognition of that power took the natural form of interpreting it as God in his heart. With his training in theistic Judaism, it could hardly have been otherwise.

We can appropriate the values of Jesus' religious experience without accepting his interpretation of that experience, just as we have a radically different scientific explanation of the disease phenomena which he interpreted as demon-possession, in common with all men of the time.

Humanists recognize that in Jesus himself lay the power which he and his followers attributed to God. That power was human and natural, not magic or supernatural. Surely the day has come when we can give up the ancient notion that unusual personalities are to be explained by interpreting their uncommon powers as due to the residence within them of a deity come down to earth.

If Jesus explained his power by saying "The Father that dwelleth in me, he doeth the works," must we necessarily accept his theistic explanation? And must we think that his explanation was as theistic as it has been made to seem by those for whom that Father is the second person of a hypothetical Trinity?

Somehow it seemed heretical to the Theists who listened to him that he located God within himself and spoke of himself as the son of God. They sensed the Humanism of such an utterance and called it just what Theists today call Humanism, blasphemy.

Blasphemy is daring to assert that the powers are in us which our forefathers have said were in a God, which their forefathers made in their own image.

If Jesus used the following frequently quoted words, have we not a right to say that his ideas were of a humanistic trend, even if he used theistic terms, and even if he believed in a personal God? Take such phrases as:

"The kingdom of God is within you."

"Greater things than these shall ye do, for I go unto the Father."

"The sabbath was made for man."

"He that hath seen me hath seen the Father."

These can all be matched with such anti-humanistic statements as, "The Father is greater than I," and "I can of mine own self do nothing."

Probably we shall be as near the truth as may be if we assert that the religion of Jesus was Theism with a humanistic flavor. It is well illustrated in a statement of his which did not get into the canonical gospels but which was discovered not long ago in the Oxyrhynchus papyrus:

> "and the kingdom of heaven is within you, and whosoever shall know himself shall find it—(Strive therefore)—to know yourself and ye shall be aware that ye are the sons of the Father."

If this is authentic, it is clearly humanistic in enjoining self-recognition and in locating heaven within.

Perhaps the theistic implication of the word Father is largely a matter of phraseology. The kinship of man to God, suggested in the word sons, implies that what has been termed divinity is, after all, accessible to human beings. This power called God is available to the sons of God. It is the natural step for those who cannot accept the supernatural to go a bit further and say that perhaps the power which comes from self-recognition is man's own power, after all, and that to attribute it to God is a circumlocution no longer necessary.

Did Jesus then believe that human personality is of supreme value and is self-perfectible? In other words, was he a Humanist?

He held human personality of great value. In even the outcasts of society he perceived great possibilities. The result of his teachings has been to increase immeasurably the world's estimate of human worth. And he urged men, "Be ye therefore perfect," but he added "as your Father in heaven is perfect."

The theistic coloring of his thought prevents Humanists from claiming him as altogether their own, but the strongly humanistic trend of many of his utterances leads them to hail him as a kindred spirit and to bring him their reverence and respect.

6 FUNDAMENTALISM, MODERNISM, AND HUMANISM

Last spring when Dr. Henry Sloan Coffin called Fundamentalists and Modernists to unite to fight Humanism, "the scourge of Christendom," he was right in recognizing the importance of the Humanist movement and the danger it is to Theism. He deserves the credit of having discovered the enemy and of having shouted the alarm, even if his words were not felicitously chosen. His phrase, "the scourge of Christendom," links Humanism with Attila the Hun or the Black Plague, but Humanists pardon the hyperbole and only beg to remind Dr. Coffin that invective is not a satisfactory permanent substitute for argument.

The trouble with Dr. Coffin's call to arms was that it should have included all orthodoxies, all religions of authority, all theistic faiths. Christians have no monopoly on Theism: their variety seems so important to them that they frequently forget that their religion is but one of many theistic faiths which are all alike shaken to their foundations by the spread of scientific knowledge among the peoples of the world.

Jewish Theists, for instance, have already revealed themselves as stout allies in the fight against Humanism, and many a synagogue has resounded with thundering denunciations of the new religion. At the same time the rabbis have, rather inconsistently, assured their hearers that no Jew need become a Humanist for Judaism contains everything that Humanism has.

It has been amusing to note the pleased but rather apprehensive surprise with which Christians have awakened to the realization that the Jews have a god strangely similar to theirs. In the new alliance of Christianity and Judaism perhaps they will both discover that the additions which the former made to the latter are not so important as they both have supposed.

Muhammadanism is in as much danger as Christianity or Judaism, for the reformation now rumbling in Islam to the alarm of the orthodox will not stop at the half-way house of a Muhammadan Modernism. It is already markedly humanistic and its leaders are preaching a religion practically identical with American religious Humanism.

Humanism is not the "scourge of Christendom" alone. It challenges all theistic orthodoxies. Not only should the civil war of Fundamentalists and Modernists cease in the presence of a common enemy, but those Theists who are proselyting in theistic lands should swiftly change their tactics and form an alliance with their former prospective converts.

Let the missionaries be called home from any land whose native religion is theistic. Let Dr. Coffin shout louder and call in all "heathen" supernaturalists to the help of beleaguered Christian Theism.

In his war against the new heresy, Dr. Coffin may even be forced to call on the Pope for help, who is supposed to be an expert in such matters. Who knows but that the menace of Humanism may unite Christendom! Vain hope, for Christians have too long fought each other over methods of baptism and the phraseology of creeds and the details of the communion service for them to be able to unite now against Humanism.

Last autumn the opening of the college year at Union Theological Seminary was signalized by an address by Dr. Harry Emerson Fosdick on The Limitations of Humanism, the substance of which appeared in the December issue of *Harpers Magazine* under the caption, "Religion without God?" This was evidently an arranged "follow-up" of Dr. Coffin's pronouncement at commencement a few months before.

Dr. Fosdick's article is the best anti-humanist document which has yet emanated from the ranks of the Modernists, but from it Humanists have nothing to fear and in it there is little to answer. In fact, there is more than a suggestion in it that Christendom needs to be "scourged," or at least humanized in its theology.

In the article the author reveals himself as already well on the way toward Humanism. He approves of much in it, he admits. The faults he finds are not the faults of the religious Humanism which he thinks he is attacking: they are the faults of the current literary or academic Humanism which is frequently confused with religious Humanism to the great annoyance of representatives of both varieties. Of this literary Humanism a statement and criticism will be made in Chapter Nine.

Dr. Fosdick's main charges against Humanism are that it is atheistic, mechanistic and does not appreciate the value of personality. Surely the great and gifted Modernist has not had much acquaintance with the utterances of the religious Humanists. Since the appearance of his article there has gone up a chorus of protest against such misjudgment.

Dr. Dieffenbach, editor of *The Christian Register* (Unitarian), speaking before a meeting of Boston Universalist ministers, November 25, mentioned the Fosdick article and said:

> "His Humanism is not the Humanism that I have seen in our fellowship. . . . All the way through his article he assumes that Humanism is necessarily atheistic and mechanistic. I don't know a single person who talks mechanistic nonsense. Even scientists have given that up. . . .
>
> "I am not alarmed about Humanism. In the future, I think there will be more of the essence of it than there will be of what we call Theism. As an editor who studies the signs of the times, I am not disturbed, because I see that the men in our fellowship who are Humanists primarily are men of spiritual fervor and builders of the kingdom of heaven on earth."

Editor Harold Buschman of *The New Humanist*, in the December 1929 issue of his magazine, criticized Dr. Fosdick's article:

> "All Humanists ought to be grateful to the Rev. Mr. Fosdick for his article in the December issue of Harpers, entitled 'Religion without God.' It ought to stand as a warning to all of us whether we are Humanists, Theists, or neither. . . . The battle of Humanism and Theism cannot be fought out along the simple lines laid down in the article. The antitheses that Mr. Fosdick projects into the controversy are, at least in the opinion of this writer, the shallow biproducts of the fundamental quest. Mechanism versus purpose, quantitative versus qualitative, machine versus personality! All these are very interesting and useful words, but of what real significance

are they in the controversy? Many leading Humanists reject any 'mechanistic theory of the universe' quite as insistently as do the Theists, and they contend just as vigorously as the Theists for qualitative sciences. And that captivating word personality turns (or does) as many tricks for some Humanists as for some Theists."

As a matter of fact, Dr. Fosdick, toward the end of his article, honestly admits what Humanists have frequently asserted, namely, that what Theists today lack, and without which they cannot successfully combat Humanism, is a satisfactory theistic definition of God.

This "positive presentation of a credible idea of God," which Dr. Fosdick admits the lack of, he also admits is not likely to be composed very soon, confessing that:

"amid the mass of undigested factual material which modern religion faces, the thoughtful Theist knows that he often appears vague in his idea of deity. He frankly despairs of tossing off on demand a statement of Theism philosophically adequate to this new amazing universe. He sees in that task work for many minds demanding more than one generation, but he is still convinced that atheism is no solution of the problem and that behind our partial and inadequate ideas of God is God."

There could be no better picture of the tragic dilemma of Modernism, the liberal wing of Christianity.

Modernism has lost its old God, is prevented by its knowledge of science from finding a new, and dreads to turn to atheism. It is time for the Fundamentalists to say, I told you so. Better a clear-cut

Fundamentalism than this sadly inadequate Modernism. Fundamentalism is based on the old pre-scientific world-view and refuses to accept evolution because evolution means the end of Christianity as it has been. The Modernists have fallen between two stools in trying to sit on both. A new faith for the new age is what we want, and Humanism is that faith.

7 THE HUMANIST ATTITUDE TOWARD PRAYER AND WORSHIP

Prayer has passed through many stages of evolution and is now entering another in which it has become something so different from its former character that it is very doubtful if we are justified in using the word prayer to describe it.

It is changing from a petition addressed to an outside deity to a meditative study of one's personality with a view to self-improvement and self-giving in intelligent service to one's fellowmen. If the latter exercise is prayer, then Humanists pray, but they prefer as more honest to describe it in other terms than prayer.

John Haynes Holmes of New York has recently presented what he calls "A Humanistic Interpretation of Prayer" (*Christian Century*, October 16, 1929). He finds three elements in prayer.

First, "It is the deliberate formulation in our minds of something that we need or want, . . . the conscious, deliberate fixation of our inner attention upon the needs and aspirations of our lives."

Second, "it is the conscious deliberate direction of our life forces to the attainment of our desires." That is, the individual determines to do all in his power to bring his desire to accomplishment, for "if our prayers are to be answered we must answer them ourselves."

Third, "the conscious and deliberate attempt to gain contact with the universe—to identify ourselves with cosmic destiny." This he considers the ultimate and highest meaning of prayer.

A wide discussion of this definition of prayer ensued in the columns of the *Christian Century;* about a thousand letters were received by the editors.

Mr. Holmes called his definition psychological rather than theological and humanistic rather than theistic, but many of his readers disagreed with him, and were sure that he was theistic and had a theology.

This interpretation of prayer really belongs to the cosmic consciousness school, and whether or not it is theistic depends upon how personal one considers cosmic destiny to be.

To formulate our needs, to direct our powers to the attainment of our desires, and to attempt to relate ourselves to the universe,—none of these needs a personal God, and all of them together are certainly not what has commonly been meant by prayer.

Classically, prayer has always presupposed a person who could hear the prayer, and if belief in a personal God is no longer possible for scientifically trained folk, then those persons obviously can no longer pray. Even one who has begun to doubt the existence of such a God ceases to pray. Prayer is a vanishing custom, even in Christian churches to say nothing of Christian homes. The Friday night or Wednesday night prayer-meeting of Protestant churches has either vanished or evolved into a lecture or discussion-group, save in a few Fundamentalist communities. The family altar and grace before meals are disappearing in spite of the frantic protests and threats of the preachers. Of course, this is deemed to be a sign of increasing worldliness and wickedness. It really indicates the passing of the personal God idea, even among those who still profess to believe in the God of their fathers.

Even the "long prayer" of the Sunday morning service of worship has been appreciably shortened within a generation. If a minister prays more than six or seven minutes (the long prayer used to be twenty minutes to a half-hour long) he is warned. If he repeats the offense, he suddenly finds that his wife's health necessitates a change of climate. Catastrophes were formerly averted by a friendly warning from a deacon during the service itself, but since hunting-case watches went out of style, the matter is more difficult.

Why do parishioners demand shorter prayers? Because they feel embarrassed and uncomfortable during the fervent address to deity. And why do they feel uncomfortable? Is it because they are sinners in the hands of an angry God? No, it is because they have been educated in a scientific age and are doubtful of the existence of even a friendly God. They go to church because they wish to be thought respectable and to support an institution which they still consider an asset to the community. But they do not propose to be tortured more than is absolutely necessary with the exercises of an outgrown theology.

In the animistic period of primitive religion, before even the gods were developed, prayer consisted in touching some sacred stone or tree, or drinking or bathing in holy waters, in order to absorb the "mana" or power resident in the sacred object. The recent Malden, Massachusetts, cemetery demonstrations, where hundreds of thousands crowded to touch the gravestone of a priest or to take handfuls of earth from his grave, were an excellent example of a survival of that primitive sort of prayer.

When the gods arrived, sacrifice and the priesthood, both closely related to prayer, developed, and prayers gradually became more definitely vocal.

The word prayer comes from the Sanskrit, *prach,* to ask, through the Latin, *precari,* to entreat or pray, and the French, *prier,* to pray.

When prayer reached the vocal stage, then, it was simply as asking, naive and direct, for what the petitioner wished. As the prayer was uttered there was presented with it some offering. We find such simple early prayers as:

"Here is butter: give us cows,"
"I vow my hair: heal my body," and, much later,
"I vow poverty and chastity: give me peace."

But the answer did not always come.

Our word precarious comes directly from the Latin, *precarius,* signifying obtained by prayer. It was early recognized that answers to prayer were very uncertain.

The priests came to the rescue. The reason why no answer had come to the earnest prayer was because the petitioner had not brought the right sacrifice, or had not approached the altar from the correct side or in the correct apparel, or had not recited the accepted formula.

Prayers then became more formal and ritualistic. Services of elaborate worship grew up in time around the act of prayer and its accompanying sacrifice. The whole service of worship, whatever it may have evolved into as an esthetic exercise, was originally

HUMANISM: A NEW RELIGION

and through countless centuries essentially a process of getting the god in good humor so as to increase the chances of getting the desired answer to the prayer.

In other words, worship is an elaboration of prayer.

Humanists neither pray nor worship in the usual sense of those words, because they think that the mental attitude involved in the act of worship or prayer is one they cannot honestly assume.

An agnostic cannot and does not wish to pray to or worship a being whose very existence he doubts, and a Humanist does not need to. All the real values of worship and prayer are available for him without his violating his conscience by pretending to believe that which he honestly cannot believe.

The values resident in worship are beauty, repose of spirit, fine music, common concentration on a high ideal, the hearing of tried and true words of scripture and of an inspiring address, and association with similarly minded people.

The values resident in prayer are meditation, aspiration, self-inventory, and high resolve.

Every one of these values is accessible to the Humanist, either in his own home or in a humanist meeting without petition to or mental prostration before a supernatural or personal deity.

It is interesting to note, in definitions of prayer and in epigrams about it, how human and natural have been the emphases. To a Humanist the following quotations contain acceptable ideas:

> "Prayer is the peace of our spirit, the stillness of our thoughts, the evenness of our recollection."—JEREMY TAYLOR.

THE HUMANIST ATTITUDE TOWARD PRAYER AND WORSHIP

"For the most part, we should pray rather in aspiration than petition, rather by hoping than requesting."—LEIGH HUNT.

"To plow is to pray: to plant is to prophesy; and the harvest answers and fulfills."
—ROBERT G. INGERSOLL.

"No man ever prayed heartily without learning something."—RALPH WALDO EMERSON.

"Prayer is a self-preached sermon."
—JEAN PAUL RICHTER.

"Prayer is the soul's sincere desire,
  Unuttered or expressed;
The motion of a hidden fire
  That trembles in the breast."
—JAMES MONTGOMERY

But why call it prayer, when prayer is by definition and common usage a verbal petition addressed to a personal deity?

In churches where they prayed for rain a generation ago, a new type of minister, college-trained and familiar with science, is insisting that prayer is really but one's "dominant desire." But if that be prayer, one does not need a God. It is embarrassing to ask a supernatural deity to break the cause-and-effect law in order to give us some particular thing we may think we need.

Prayer is superseded for the Humanist by personality-development, and that requires self-study, a knowledge of psychology and other sciences, the training of desire, and the cultivation of character, rather than a sacred magic formula addressed to a deity in the skies.

8 THE PROBLEM OF IMMORTALITY

If immortality means surviving after death as an influence in the lives of those who live after us, or if it means surviving biologically in our children, then of course Humanists believe in immortality. There is inspiration for right living in both these conceptions and many noble souls have looked forward to no other immortality.

But immortality has usually meant the continuance of human personality after death in an ideal society apart from the earth.

This concept contains two elements, the idea of an ideal society and the idea of personal survival. The two have been so blended in the Christian tradition that it is difficult to separate them in our thinking, but in some religions the two are not so equally present. Sometimes one is emphasized and sometimes the other. They rise from different sources.

The idea of an ideal society in the future naturally rises when men are hindered from building the society here. The oppressed classes see no hope of justice in this life and they look for it in the next. A blissful heaven is a compensatory hope in a world of misery. Men have looked forward to many mansions in their heavenly Father's land when their hearts were troubled and afraid here. Happy hunting grounds, the islands of the blest, the golden age to come, the Muhammadan paradise,—many have been the forms that man's imagination has chosen as the ideal place of final abode for man. All that weary mankind has failed to find on this earth it has hoped to find after death in some fairer clime.

Humanists sympathize with such a desire for a perfect home for man, but hold that the ideal society is to be achieved on this earth if anywhere.

They maintain, moreover, that the expectation of finding the perfect society in heaven is a distinct hindrance to the achievement of a better society on this earth.

The real heaven-hunters have no interest in improving the conditions here. To a Humanist the beliefs of the Fundamentalists who hope for the speedy return of Jesus on the clouds of heaven seem positively immoral. In their frenzy the millenialists hail with joy the news of famine, pestilence, "wars and rumors of wars," for such catastrophes are portents that the end is near. The worse things get, the better, for the sooner Jesus will come! These are the "latter days" and "millions now living will never die." So why do anything to make the earth better: it will only delay the millenium.

Two leading preachers of New York City who continually featured in their sermons the imminent return of the Lord, refused to cooperate in a child welfare program, saying frankly that they had no time to waste on the fads of social reformers as they were too busy saving souls from the wrath to come.

Even in those Protestant circles where adventism is not so strongly emphasized, the stress has too frequently been laid on preparing for the next world. Christians have sung lustily, "I'm a pilgrim and I'm a stranger," "I'm but a stranger here: heaven is my home," "Sometime we'll understand," "When the roll is called up yonder," "Jerusalem the golden," "Safe in the arms of Jesus," "Beulah Land," and a hundred other similar hymns. Meanwhile unscrupulous men have taken advantage of the absorption of the righteous in the next world and have exploited them and their children. And a world war that could have been prevented loomed nearer and nearer while the Christian nations who were to wage it sat in their churches and heard sermons about the coming glories of heaven.

Dr. A. Eustace Haydon, in *The Quest of the Ages*, (p. 156) recently wrote:

> "With the coming of modern science and the new age of industry, the result of the projection of the religious ideal to another world was tragic. It allowed the whole mechanism of modern civilization to develop without the control of religious idealism."

So, inasmuch as the existence of heaven is at least debatable and its location problematical since we have studied astronomy, Humanists make the suggestion that we assume the agnostic position in regard to heaven and devote our energies to improving our imperfect planet.

The second element in the concept of immortality, the idea of personal survival, is popularly, but not necessarily, connected with the first element, the idea of an ideal society into which the individual may be inducted after his decease. A person might conceivably survive after death without going to a heaven. It might be a neutral sort of place, like the Hebrew Sheol or the Greek Hades. It might be a bad place, like hell. Or the immortal soul might wander alone

THE PROBLEM OF IMMORTALITY

as a ghost in far spaces, or even return unseen to his former haunts.

The origin of the idea of personal survival has had several explanations, but the ghost theory seems as plausible as any. It seems likely that very early in human history men must have developed the idea of immortality, because primitive graves contain food and weapons for the departed warrior to use in the next life.

When a man visited a place where he had often walked with a friend recently dead, he naturally recalled their companionship there. It seemed as if the friend were still with him. Perhaps he was still there, but invisible, a ghost. In other words, a person who survived in memory was supposed to have survived in some non-corporeal form, invisible but really present.

If that were so, early man argued, then all the dead must be around their old haunts. It gave the living a sense of awe and fear to think that their old friends and relatives might be still around them, possibly influencing their lives in unseen ways. Elaborate methods of pleasing the good ghosts and of placating the evil ones developed and were incorporated into religion.

But Humanists have little belief in spirits, and think that the survival of the individual is based on flimsy foundations if it has no other evidence for it than the suppositions of primitive, fearful, and superstitious folk.

That is not to say that Humanists would dismiss without examination the evidence submitted by societies for psychical research. Cleansed of charlatanry and self-deception, psychical research, scientifically conducted, may afford preliminary observations and experimental data concerning this as yet little understood thing called human personality.

Here again, the Humanist is agnostic, but open-minded. He thinks that evidence of survival, if any such evidence exists, is more likely to be discovered by the developed science of tomorrow when it seriously turns its attention to the study of unusual personality phenomena, psychic and otherwise, than by revealed religion.

Believing as he does, that human personality is of supreme value, and self-perfectible, the Humanist will not assume any dogmatic position against immortality, if immortality is conceived as a state of improved and perfected personality.

There have been three crises in evolution thus far: first, when matter took on the form of life; second, when life developed mind; third, when mind became conscious of itself.

The fourth crisis may be upon us now, and it may be what people mean when they talk about immortality. If the third crisis was when the animal, man, achieved self-recognition, when he became conscious of himself as a self, perhaps the fourth crisis is the recognition by man of his potential immortality.

But the word immortality is so inadequate. It has been used with such time and space connotations, life-everlasting and heaven, that we hesitate to use it for what the Humanist would substitute for the old concepts of immortality.

For when man has asserted his immortality, he has been simply using the best words and thought-concepts he had to express his confidence in the supreme value of his own personality.

THE PROBLEM OF IMMORTALITY

When a Humanist is asked if he believes in immortality, he may answer that he doesn't need to, for he has something better. The Theist has sometimes expressed the idea of immortality quantitatively, by saying it means endless life. The Humanist regards the time element as not so important, the quality of life being a higher consideration.

Again, the Theist has defined immortality as living in an ideal society beyond the grave. The Humanist prefers to try to build it on this earth.

Still again, the Theist has defined immortality as living with God. The Humanist replies that God is but the personification of humanity's highest ideals, and that the circumlocution is unnecessary and confusing.

Immortality has too often been considered a state into which a person is suddenly inducted. Now he is mortal and the next minute immortal. Such dualism is not consistent with the Humanist's idea of the unity of life.

The Humanist substitutes for immortality, what? Faith in the supreme value and self-perfectibility of human personality. When mankind comes to that faith, it will be seen that the idea of immortality was an interesting but temporary method of asserting man's supreme worth.

And the recognition by man of the infinite possibilities of human personality, of itself and by itself, is the fourth crisis of evolution. We shall arrive at that period as soon as we dare to believe in ourselves, individually and socially, and when we do we shall be what we used to call immortal, and we shall find a better word for it.

9 IS HUMANISM A RELIGION?

There are two objections made to considering Humanism a religion.

One is based on the assertion that since religion is by its very nature a belief in the supernatural, Humanism cannot be a religion, for it rejects the supernatural. That objection has been already answered in the first chapter.

The other objection is made by those who identify modern Humanism with a school of literary criticism embodying a sort of humanistic philosophy.

There would be no objection to having two contemporary manifestations of the same humanistic spirit, one in religion and the other in a philosophy of culture. One would strengthen the other.

But, unfortunately, the academic Humanists and the religious Humanists are birds of decidedly different feather.

The academic Humanists go back to the Greek Humanists for their name, but what they take from Greek Humanism besides the name is not the characteristic attitude associated with that great group of leaders of Hellenistic culture. Instead of taking over that bold, sweeping spirit of free inquiry, of agnostic, even free-thinking opposition to supernaturalism, of heretical assertion that man himself is the measure of all things, these modern academic Humanists are content to appropriate simply the poise and equanimity which was the result of that freedom.

IS HUMANISM A RELIGION?

Professor Irving Babbitt, in the February 1930 issue of the *Forum,* says:

> "This older (Grecian) tradition may be defined as humanistic. The goal of the Humanist is poised and proportionate living. . . . Decorum is supreme for the Humanist even as humility takes precedence over all other virtues in the eyes of the Christian."

The article proceeds to extol the virtues of decorum and humility as the marks of the academic humanistic Christian gentleman. The article is captioned, "What I Believe, by Irving Babbitt, America's Chief Exponent of Humanism."

The particular target of the article is Rousseau, the great Encyclopedist, who helped mightily to keep the spirit of Humanism flaming bright in the eighteenth century.

It is easily seen that there is a difference between the central emphases of academic and religious Humanism today. In the preface to a bibliography of Humanism now in preparation by Sherman D. Wakefield the distinction between the two is drawn as follows:

> "Academic or Classical Humanism is to be sharply distinguished from Religious Humanism. The former is concerned with a limited field of human life, while the latter takes as its motto the words of Terence: 'I am a man, and nothing human is foreign to me.' The former says Humanism is not a religion, although often making a religion of its own little field, while the latter says Humanism is the only complete religion. The Academic Humanist lives in the past, while the Religious Humanist lives supremely in the present and is looking toward the future. The

former is a Platonist rather than an Aristotelian, a Supernaturalist rather than a Naturalist, an Idealist rather than a Realist, and a Dualist rather than a Monist, as Religious Humanists generally are. His studies are Language, Literature and Art, the 'Humanities,' rather than the sciences, and his academic degree is B.A. rather than B.S., whereas the Religious Humanist accepts not only the arts but makes science his technique of control for the attainment of the good life."

Another version of alleged Humanism is found in Joseph Wood Krutch's book, *The Modern Temper*. Now Mr. Krutch is "too radical religiously and scientifically to be an Academic Humanist and too pessimistic for the future of man to be a Religious Humanist," to quote Mr. Wakefield further. In fact, he is not really a Humanist at all, but he has been taken to represent Humanism by many critics of it, including Dr. Fosdick, so he must be mentioned.

Mr. Krutch finds the world "an unresolvable discord." No escape exists. All we can do is to make "what peace we may." "Ours is a lost cause and there is no place for us in the natural universe, yet we are not, for all that, sorry to be human. We should rather die as men than live as animals."

Rarely has naturalism been carried to such extremes. What has happened to Mr. Krutch is that he has lost the illusions of supernatural Theism and has not found a new faith. The answer made to *The Modern Temper* by Dr. A. Eustace Haydon is an offer of the new faith, religious Humanism, which will afford not only Mr. Krutch but also many other baffled moderns a living scientific religion for the

IS HUMANISM A RELIGION?

twentieth century. Dr. Haydon writes, in *The New Humanist,* January 1930, as follows:

> "The criticism which Mr. Krutch makes of Humanism, of science, of art, and morals shows clearly that his eyes are turned wistfully toward the lost Atlantis of absolute, eternal security where man walked the earth in divine dignity crowned with the halo of immortality. That there is a new Humanism which has slain his dragons and faces the future with a quiet gladness he does not seem to know. His criticism of science takes no account of the fact that science has not yet been humanized, that it has not yet been set intelligently to the task of serving a deliberately chosen human ideal. . . . There must be a synthesis of scientific techniques in the science of human ends which will make the values of living actual for the millions. That this has not yet been achieved ought not to surprise one who has evidently not yet realized that man must assume responsibility for weaving purpose and beauty into the growing structure of the world."

Mr. Walter Lippmann, in his *Preface to Morals,* approached the dreary morass in which Mr. Krutch is mired, but saved himself by the discovery of high religion, which is essentially the religious Humanism of which we have been speaking, for he identifies high religion with matured personality, saying (p. 193):

> "I venture, at least, to suggest that the function of high religion is to reveal to men the quality of mature experience, that high religion is a prophecy and an anticipation of what life is like when desire is in perfect harmony with reality. It announces the discovery that men can enter into the realm of the spirit when they have outgrown all childishness."

HUMANISM: A NEW RELIGION

But Mr. Lippmann and Mr. Krutch are rejected as Humanists by the main body of academic Humanists in the symposium edited by Norman Foerster, entitled *Humanism and America,* including contributions by Irving Babbitt, Paul Elmer More, and T. S. Eliot. It seems that Messrs. Lippmann and Krutch are too revolutionary and that "The New Humanism is Revolt against Revolt—the keynote of culture for the 1930's."

The Foerster, More, Babbitt group of academic Humanists opposes with vehemence both the extreme naturalism of Krutch and also the belief in man and the revolt against supernaturalism which characterizes the religious Humanists.

The academic Humanists deserve applause for their defense of the dignity and integrity of the individual in this day of success-worship and standardization. With them on that issue the religious Humanists gladly stand. But academic Humanism of the type represented in this symposium is alarmist in temper, orthodox in tendency and likely to degenerate into a new scholasticism. Much that is human is alien to it.

Is Humanism a religion? It is both a religion and a philosophy of culture. Academic or classical Humanists and religious Humanists both have a right to the name, but if they wish to avoid misunderstandings, they will both do well to prefix a qualifying adjective to the word Humanism.

10 WHAT INSPIRATION DOES HUMANISM OFFER THE INDIVIDUAL?

The humanist attitude toward God and prayer and immortality seems to a Theist destructive of all inspiration in religion. Theists are continually asking what help such a religion can give to a man from whom it has taken away his traditional beliefs.

When the question is asked, What inspiration can Humanism offer if it rejects the supernatural?, the Humanist replies by asking what inspiration the supernatural can possibly be to an intelligent, educated person today.

The inspirations of Humanism are the twin visions of an ideal developed human personality and an ideal commonwealth made up of such persons. Dr. John Dewey, the great humanist educator, calls it "dynamic social idealism."

If the Theist asks where he shall go for comfort in time of trouble if he has no personal God to whom to pray, the Humanist answers:

"You have all the real help you ever had. There is just as much help available now, and more, only you will no longer deceive yourself as to its source, and you will use a different technique in getting it."

"But God did help me," insists the Theist.

"You mean you were helped," replies the Humanist. "You went to a quiet room and expressed your desires. The very expression gave you relief and cleared the issue in your mind. After quiet meditation on the problem, your duty became clear; you saw matters in their true perspective; you resolved to do your best, and peace came to your troubled mind. In other words, you called on your own reserves, and from the depths of your own personality help came. You went back to your work refreshed and comforted in spirit and you said that God helped you. Yet the only person in the room all the time was yourself."

"But why do you take away my God?" complains the Theist.

And the Humanist answers in the words of Schopenhauer, "To free a man from error is to give, not to take away."

There is a hard transition to be made by those who come from a dependent Theism to an independent Humanism. It requires a real conversion, a reversal of the old conversion which required a man to give up his will and simply "trust and obey." Humanism asks a man to develop his consciousness of his own resources and to believe in humanity's ability to make this world better. There arrives then what a young Humanist, Rev. Alfred W. Hobart of Chicago, recently called "that almost mystical joy which comes of the conviction of humanity's dependence upon itself." Dr. Dietrich says:

> "Here is a world blundering and bruising itself, wasting its superb resources, weakened and impoverished by disunion and strife, and we believe that in its place can be built a world more uniformly sunny and joyous, a world united and skilfully organized, a world free from illusions and superstitions, a world proud of its developed

strength and wisdom and creativeness. . . .
This is indeed a faith that should put fire into
the bones of every man who loves his kind. What
else in all the world is worthwhile if only an era
of individual and social righteousness can be
established upon earth, and life can be made desirable to the whole of mankind?"

By what method does Humanism hope to accomplish this greatest of all tasks?

The cultivation of personality and the development of the consciousness of man must begin with the individual but in cooperation with the personalities of other individuals working together in as great a degree of harmony as possible, each individual like a separate instrument in a great symphony, each contributing and developing his part, but conscious of being a factor in a great whole.

To this end there must exist an atmosphere of goodwill among men, or the friction of misunderstanding will destroy the harmony and inhibit the development of the individual.

With the awakening of consciousness in the universe, the individual became aware of the existence of other individuals. These other individuals must naturally have been considered as enemies. Driven by his own urge, he discovered himself to be seriously limited by the aggressiveness of the urge in other individuals.

Conscious of the power of force in the universe, and cognizant of the fact that his neighbor possessed urge as well as himself, primitive man loved neither his god by which he personified power, nor his neighbor, but feared both.

From a sense of dependence upon his god and a

sense of interdependence with his neighbor man discovered that he must come to some sort of terms with both. Ill will began to become good will. Man began to love his neighbor and his god. He learned too that he must first learn to love his neighbor whom he hath seen before he could love God whom he hath not seen.

So necessary is love and goodwill to the development of human consciousness that the highest conception of God that man has yet postulated is God as love, but it means only that man continues to make personal his highest ideal.

But love is not power nor an attribute of power. The "power of love" cannot be taken literally.

Love is a product of the flowering of human personality and can exist only between personalities. That love is an attribute of God according to theistic conception is consistent because God to them is a person though spiritual.

Man needs love and goodwill, both toward his fellowman and for his own self-development. Fear and misunderstanding must be removed. In the spirit of altruism must man carry on his task of personality development.

Every man will assume the responsibility for his own development but pledge himself that his efforts shall be in accordance with the best interests of the development of mankind.

Man will interest himself in all departments of life that contribute to the upbuilding of personality and will consider it his responsibility to further actively all such causes, as far as and in such ways as he is able. Instead of consecrating his life to the service of God and to the saving of souls in order

WHAT INSPIRATION DOES HUMANISM OFFER THE INDIVIDUAL?

to add stars to his own crown in a life hereafter, he will believe that all things work together for good to those who really love man. Strong in that faith he will go forward joyous in the conscious power of his developing personality, gathering new energy to push on through the no-man's land of ignorance toward the goal of complete and perfected personality to which all mankind aspires.

(The question has been asked, What is the difference between Humanism and Ethical Culture? It is obvious here that ethical culture is a means to an end in Humanism and might be considered a department of Humanism.)

Humanists believe that life is abundantly worthwhile, and that character counts, and that character is achieved by studying one's tendencies, correcting wrong trends and encouraging good ones, developing one's personality by acquiring knowledge and wisdom, by avoiding the lesser good and choosing the right path even though it be rugged, by generous self-giving to worthy causes, by faith in the possibilities of human nature, and by treating others as we should like them to treat us.

> "Sits there no judge in heaven our sin to see?—
> More strictly, then, the inner judge obey.
> Was Christ a man like us?—Ah, let us try
> If we then, too, can be such men as he!"

The distress of mind and the fear of loss of inspiration and hope disappear from the timid convert to Humanism when he realizes that giving up the God-idea or becoming agnostic about it does not mean that one surrenders the predicates of God.

The idea of God has had a certain value in the

119

past, altogether apart from the question as to whether such a God ever existed. The functional value of the God-idea must be kept separate from debates about the reality back of it.

This point is easily seen when we compare the God-idea with the Santa Claus idea. There is a certain period in the early life of the child when Santa Claus is a very real person to him. He thinks of the genial Santa as the very personification of generosity and goodwill. When the child grows older and discovers that Santa Claus is not a real person, it is a disappointment to him, but he learns after a while to make the adjustment. He discovers that loss of faith in Santa does not mean that one loses faith in generosity and goodwill.

In a similar fashion, those who wean themselves, sometimes with many heart-aches, from the God of their youth, discover that they are not necessarily losing the values formerly personified in their idea of God.

Among those values which the idea of God offered believers were 1) an explanation of how the world and man came to exist, 2) a sense of relation to the universe, 3) a sense of protection, 4) an ideal to strive toward, 5) a means of social control, 6) a mystic sense of union with the divine, 7) a feeling that all would be well after death.

The Humanist believes that all these values formerly conserved in the God-idea are available today without any faith in supernaturalism. The first two, for instance, are supplied by the theory of evolution. As for a sense of protection, the things against which man prayed to be protected, such as hunger, poverty, and sickness, are now better avoided by human agencies. Man does not need as much protection as formerly and is growing self-confident enough to take pride in doing his own protecting of himself.

For an ideal to strive toward, the Humanist looks to a completed personality in an ideal social state.

Instead of the fear of God as a means of social control, man prefers the goodwill of man. He considers the humanistic Golden Rule much better than the Ten Commandments.

For a mystic sense of union with the divine, the Humanist substitutes a genuine reverence for and appreciation of truth, beauty and goodness, as found in nature, including human nature.

Finally, the Humanist has no fear of death. Much of the fear of death from which Theism is supposed to save a man has been created by Theism itself.

All the values of the God-idea are available to the Humanist from other sources.

Those Theists among the clergy who are rather doubtful of the historicity of God and who still retain the God-idea for its functional value—for other people—forget that the clergy are no longer the only learned ones. He who would save God so that the masses may have someone to lean on cannot be aware of the democracy of learning. The truth cannot be kept away from modern folk. And how many persons, educated or not, are going to retain the idea of God for its functional value after they have come to doubt the existence of God?

The question, therefore, is not, as some seem to think it is, What shall we give the people in exchange for their faith in God? The ones who still believe in a deity are not looking for an exchange. The question is, What inspiration is there in Humanism for those who have abandoned Theism? And the answer is, the abundant inspiration of the belief that the man who created gods for himself in his racial childhood can in his maturity create a satisfactory human society.

11 THE SOCIAL PROGRAM OF HUMANISM

Humanism is frequently confused with humanitarianism.

Humanism includes humanitarian measures in its social program, but includes much more. Humanitarianism, as it is understood today, is another word for philanthropy. It has to do with alleviating the condition of the unfortunate.

The difference between humanitarianism and Humanism can be illustrated by stating that the Good Samaritan performed a humanitarian act when he bound up the wounds of the traveller and took him to an inn. The "oil and wine" which he poured into the sufferer's wounds were a primitive sort of first aid, and the inn became a temporary hospital.

But Humanism would go farther.

It would see to the policing of the Jericho road, else the next trip the Good Samaritan made he would find another wounded traveller. As a matter of startling fact, the Jericho road was not policed until the latter part of the nineteenth century! How much needless suffering there must have been, and what a hindrance to commerce!

And Humanism would not be content with policing the road. It would inquire into social and economic conditions to discover why there were robbers on that road, and would probably find that the excessive taxes demanded by the grafting tax-collectors had driven men to highway robbery in order to feed their families.

Merely Good Samaritans are not sufficient any longer. We need better Samaritans. It may have been considered a good deed in Bible times to give to all who asked and not to turn away from any would-be borrowers, but either act is now deemed detrimental to society.

What is the social program of Humanism and what its guiding principle?

Humanism favors any movement which tends to improve human personality and opposes any which degrades it.

Dr. Dietrich has put it this way:

> "Every institution—the state, the church, the school, the corporation, the labor union; and every social process—marriage, suffrage, immigration, prohibition, banking—stands or falls according to its contribution to human life. Does it foster, enlarge, liberate, ennoble the lives of men? Then it stands justified and calls for protection and support. Does it weaken, enslave, impoverish, degrade human life? Then it stands condemned and should be destroyed. Human life is the thing of supreme worth in the world, and must be treated as the end of all human endeavor. This is the corner-stone of the religion of Humanism."

According to that principle, then, Humanism would advocate the following reforms:

1. The cultivation of international and interracial amity.

2. The legalizing of birth control.
3. The improvement and extension of education.
4. The raising of cultural standards.
5. The correlation of cultural agencies.
6. The defense of freedom of speech.
7. The encouragement of art, music, drama, the dance, and all other means of self-expression.
8. The elevation of the ethical standards of moving pictures.
9. The promotion of public health.
10. The checking of standardization in cases where it injures the individual.
11. The improvement of methods of dealing with criminals.
12. The improvement of means of communicacation.
13. The abolition of religious subsidies.
14. The improvement of industrial conditions.
15. The extension of social insurance.
16. The establishment of full sex equality.
17. The extension of child welfare measures.
18. The purification of politics.
19. The abolition of special privilege.
20. The conservation of natural resources for the people.
21. The substitution of temperance for prohibition.

The methods of securing the accomplishment of these measures will naturally vary. Some require agitation; some, the education of public opinion; some, demonstration. It will be many years before they can be accomplished, even with patient persistent effort, but to do this, always in a fair and open-minded attitude, is the task and the privilege of the Humanist.

Simply to list the reforms needed is to challenge the lovers of mankind to a new missionary crusade.

12 HUMANISM AND THE RELIGION OF THE FUTURE

All religions today are becoming humanistic and tomorrow they will be more so. The trend has been slow in starting but it has already acquired such a momentum that there is no stopping it. Its progress is uneven. The stream of Humanism encounters the obstacles of old orthodoxies and modern lethargies round which it must make its way until they gradually melt in its warm current.

It is in America that the destinies of the world are being shaped and in America Humanism is growing and bound to grow. Rev. E. Stanton Hodgin of New Bedford in a sermon in the volume of *Humanist Sermons* edited by Dr. Reese (p. 60), said:

> "Our nation followed a diametrically opposite course (from that of Europe). It disestablished the church, letting theology shift for itself. It in no sense repudiated religion, only declaring it to be an individual matter and no concern of the state. In place of the church that it had disestablished, it established the school, giving it state aid and authority, thus making education, human wisdom, knowledge of the world forces that impinge upon us the bulwark of national security and stability. This nation thus committed its life to the humanistic position long before such a faith was thought of as a religion. As a matter of fact, religion in its most nascent form is seldom ever recognized as religion at all."

HUMANISM: A NEW RELIGION

Education is thus a most powerful ally of Humanism, and every American public school is a school of Humanism. What can the theistic Sunday-schools, meeting for an hour once a week, and teaching only a fraction of the children, do to stem the tide of a five-day program of humanistic teaching?

The Pope and the Fundamentalists see the danger to Theism. The former would have all Catholic parents send their children to parochial schools where they can be given theistic antidotes to counteract the humanist poison so prevalent in American life! The Fundamentalists concentrate their opposition on the theory of evolution, sensing that there lies a great danger to theistic religion.

So very humanistic is modern education that no religion has a future unless it be Humanism. The religion of tomorrow in America and of the day after tomorrow in all the world may not be in all respects identical with the religious Humanism we are advocating in this book, but it will be mightily like it and of the same spirit.

One American educator, Dr. John Dewey, from whom the new type of modern education received its impetus and much of its method, and who is also best acquainted with the progress of education round the world, has this to say (*Forum*, March 1930) of great interest to all who are studying religious Humanism and the future of religion:

> "I would suggest that the future of religion is connected with the possibility of developing a faith in the possibilities of human experience and human relationships that will create a vital sense

of the solidarity of human interests and inspire action to make that sense a reality."

There stands the hope and program of religious Humanism in a single pregnant sentence.

Not only public school education is an ally of Humanism: science itself is its mother. Said Rev. Edwin H. Wilson (*The New Humanist*, April, 1929):

> "The fact is that what we are calling Humanism is a subtle, permeating influence growing organically out of the progress of scientific knowledge wherever that knowledge is effectively related to human life."

What needs to be done to science if it is to accomplish its proper service for the growth of Humanism is to correlate all human knowledge and synthesize it that it may adequately serve human ends. This is a tremendous task, but agencies are already at work to that end.

The Institute of Human Relations at Yale University is the most important agency now in the field. The Institute finds its origin in the "need for coöperation among the various branches of study which bear on the major problems of human welfare," and its end in bringing "together in a common enterprise individuals now working in correlative but separate fields of research and teaching." The various groups concerned with human relations are divided into three sections: the first, those treating of man as a physical organism; the second, those studying individual human personality; and third, those dealing with community life. These three groups will cooperate in a common research program.

This well-endowed and wisely planned enterprise will hereafter be looked back upon as one of the first great steps in creative civilization.

Both the American Council of Learned Societies and its member, the American Philosophical Society, are doing a valuable service in endeavoring to bring about a synthesis between the old "humanities" and the new social sciences. If this results in the humanizing of the humanities, let us all rejoice. Such a combining of branches of learning will mean a much-needed "intellectual stocktaking" and the making available to all workers in philosophic and literary fields the resources of knowledge now housed in various bureaus, foundations, and societies. Man is beginning to develop social self-recognition, to learn what are his resources for the great march of humanistic progress.

Education and science are on the side of Humanism. The third great power of our time is democracy, and its relation to Humanism is obvious. Democracy is the extension of political rule to the people that they may govern themselves. Democracy in government means the abolition of kings and all political autocracies. Democracy in religion means the abolition of all spiritual autocracies. A nation which has democracy in the political sphere cannot forever retain the idea of monarchy in religion.

A NOTE ON THE HUMANIST SOCIETY

The First Humanist Society of New York was founded in September, 1929. An office was opened in the Steinway Building as Humanist Headquarters and the first public meeting was held Sunday morning, September 29th, in a hall in the same building. The hall proved too small and on the third Sunday the society met in its present location in Chalif Hall, 163 West 57th Street.

The interest spread rapidly. Newspapers and magazines carried columns of publicity, much of it inaccurate in its conception of what it was all about, but of sufficient appeal to cause many citizens of various communities to ask for the establishing of branch societies.

The correspondence indicates that many people in America are ready for such a religion. There seems also to be considerable interest abroad, especially in England and India.

The plans of the New York Society include the formation of an international Humanist Union, to serve as an information center and publication headquarters for the movement.

A magazine called *The New Humanist,* definitely devoted to the cause of Humanism in religion, has been for two years published in Chicago by a group of theological students.

Dr. Curtis W. Reese of Chicago, author of *Humanism* (1926), also published in 1927 a volume of sermons by eighteen Humanists, all Unitarian preachers save two, Rev. John Haynes Holmes of New York and Dr. A. Eustace Haydon, professor of Comparative Religion in the University of Chicago.

Dr. Haydon has recently published an admirable exposition of Humanism, *The Quest of the Ages*. Two other Humanist professors have enriched the literature of the subject, Professor Roy Wood Sellars of Michigan, *Religion Coming of Age,* and Professor M. C. Otto of Wisconsin, *Things and Ideals*.

A NOTE ABOUT THE AUTHOR

Charles Francis Potter is perhaps one of the four or five leading American preachers. For eleven years he preached in the Baptist Church and for eleven more in the Unitarian. He attained national renown as the opponent of Dr. John Roach Straton in a series of debates on fundamentalism at Carnegie Hall several years ago. He was also Bible expert and Librarian for the Defense in the Scopes Evolution Trial in Dayton, Tennessee. Last year The Inner Sanctum issued The Story of Religion, *Mr. Potter's account of the lives and faiths of the greater religious leaders.*
Last Spring, Mr. Potter's beliefs, as enunciated from his pulpit in the Church of the Divine Paternity, came into conflict with the views of the church executives. His liberal views were rejected and at that time he announced that he would form an independent religious society. The First Humanist Society of New York was the result.